'As someone who works in a charity which had for some time been thinking how helpf for our clients to work through that would g illustrated by a story to guide them through their grief journey. When I read Jane's book I knew that I'd found it. Her style of writing is warm, accessible and so down to earth. Through sharing her own experience of four miscarriages with compassion and tenderness, Jane draws alongside like a friend who deeply understands. Her story contains experiences that will resonate with others who have suffered a loss during pregnancy and help them connect or reconnect with the One who holds them through it all. Written from a Christian perspective, she shares how the losses affected her, including her relationship with God, and shares Scriptures that helped her. Written as a journal for 30 days, each chapter encourages a personal response. Like a ray of light in a dark place this book offers a helpful and healing guide through difficult times.'

Letitia Ash-Lameer, former Head of Counselling, TimeNorfolk

'In this book, Jane invites the reader to join her on a 30-day journey where the pain and bewilderment of miscarriage is explored. It is honest, full of compassion and wisdom, not seeking to provide easy answers but always pointing to God who is faithful. I love its conversational style, which makes it a joy to read, and I wish there had been a book like this when I experienced my own baby losses. I highly recommend it as a resource for helping those who have had to say goodbye too soon.'

Jenny Baines, Consultant for OPEN, a ministry of CARE

Jane Clamp is an interior designer with a heart for restoration, which is also reflected in her writing and speaking ministry. She broadcasts regularly on BBC Radio Norfolk and Premier Christian Radio, and blogs for Network Norwich and the Association of Christian Writers.

TOO SOON

*A mother's journey through miscarriage:
a 30-day devotional*

Jane Clamp

First published in Great Britain in 2018

Society for Promoting Christian Knowledge
36 Causton Street
London SW1P 4ST
www.spck.org.uk

British Library Cataloguing-in-Publication Data
A catalogue record for this book is available from the British Library

ISBN 978–0–281–08027–4
eBook ISBN 978–0–281–08028–1

1 3 5 7 9 10 8 6 4 2

Typeset by Manila Typesetting Company
Printed in Great Britain by Ashford Colour Press

eBook by Manila Typesetting Company

Produced on paper from sustainable forests

Dedicated to those waiting up ahead:
Emily, Lydia, Andrew and Lily

Contents

Foreword   ix

Preface   xi

Acknowledgements   xiii

Days

  1 My baby was real   1

  2 Stop! I want to get off!   5

  3 How are you?   9

  4 Strengthen yourself in the Lord 1   12

  5 Strengthen yourself in the Lord 2   16

  6 Duvet days   19

  7 Psalm 39   22

  8 The kindness of God   25

  9 To be honest . . .   28

10 The rescue mission   32

11 Mornings of joy   35

12 No fear   38

Contents

13 Questions, questions   42

14 Psalm 41   46

15 Have a day off!   49

16 Time   51

17 In the secret place   55

18 Turning the water off   58

19 Stormy weather   61

20 The green-eyed monster   66

21 Psalm 42   70

22 Morning glory   73

23 Mother's Day   76

24 It takes two   79

25 Job's comforters   83

26 Due date   86

27 Always something to remind me   90

28 Psalm 116   93

29 Hoping for a rainbow   96

30 The end of the road   101

Liturgy for saying goodbye   105

Resources   108

Bible acknowledgements   109

Foreword

I don't believe anyone can possibly understand the pain of a miscarriage until they have had one themselves. If it is followed by several more the pain becomes unbearable, yet so often there is no one you can trust to share the depths of how you feel. That is why this book is so powerful. Jane understands exactly through her own personal experience.

I so well remember the tactless remarks from people who made bright cheerful comments such as, 'Just start another one, dear,' or worse, 'I don't know why you are making so much fuss; it was only a lump of jelly!' It is impossible to explain that the moment you know you are pregnant that 'lump of jelly' becomes a living person to you; as you lie in the bath you imagine those little buds developing into arms and legs and 'watch' the tiny heart beginning to beat. You already picture him or her starting school, winning sports day races, getting married – and the dreams go on for ever! Every year on 31 August, I catch myself working out how old my baby would be now and wondering how life might be treating the child I was sure was a boy. I can't seem to stop myself reliving the shock of discovering those bloodstains and feeling those dreaded tummy cramps. Maybe I would not still be processing that loss if I had known someone else who had experienced a miscarriage and would have let me talk about what I was going through. How very helpful this book would have been to me then.

I think a whole long book might have been too overwhelming for me to have handled back then, so I just love the way Jane has divided the pain of this experience into 30 manageable chunks to be spaced over 30 days. The prayers she has added are so sensitive and 'down to earth' that I am sure they will help people who are grieving to respond without becoming overwhelmed. The very fact Jane has talked about this experience in the format of a devotional book is brilliant because one of the most troublesome parts about having a miscarriage, particularly if it is followed by several more, is not only lack of support from other people but a sense of being abandoned by God as well. After all is said and done, he could well have prevented all this – but for some reason, which he won't explain, he failed to do so. That sense of deep disappointment and disillusionment is hard to bear and even harder for other people to understand. I love the gentle way Jane handles these tricky issues and with those prayers at the end of each day she carefully brings us back to trusting that God really can work all things around for our good (Romans 8.28).

If you have a friend or relative who is going through the grief of a miscarriage, you may well have no idea how to comfort her, perhaps because you have never had that experience yourself. You long to say something but you are afraid of 'getting it wrong' and adding to her misery. Sending her this book would definitely be a silent and very loving way of standing with her. Well done, Jane. This book was so well worth writing!

Jennifer Rees Larcombe

Preface

Twenty-one years ago I gave birth to my second son, but before his arrival I had officially lost four babies in pregnancy through miscarriage. All of them gone too soon. It was a time of hideous grief, and although the years have passed I can recall it all as if it were still happening. I've got through it – I mean, I had no choice, really – but it's fair to say I haven't got over it. As with every matter of the heart, every great love affair, I believe there is an imprint that is still visible if you angle it into the light. And what greater love is there than that of a mother for her child?

There are so many losses we suffer through life, changes that we have no control over. I can't bring back my lost children – although I believe with all my heart that they are waiting in heaven for me to join them one day – but I can decide how I want to remember them, and how they should shape my life. I may not have held them in my arms but their grip on my heart is eternal.

I am a private person when it comes to sharing my feelings, and that season of miscarriage was all the more difficult because I struggled to talk about it with those around me. Shining through the fog of those years are the memories of those who had also suffered the loss of a child; friends whose secrets had never been shared until our joint grief allowed a connection. Weeping on the shoulder of a friend who had suffered a cot death felt safe. There was no need for words, and the poor ones I could offer were understood without judgement.

There will be days, you know, when you can't hold it together, when you can't be polite or self-controlled or nice. And it's in those moments that you need someone you can rant at until the anger has passed for now and you can be calm again.

May I be that friend for you? As we meet each day in the pages of this book, please feel free to yell and shout and cry or just agree with a 'me too'! Within those expressions of honesty is freedom from which, in time, healing can come. You will not always feel as bad as you do right now, but while you do, please know that you're not going through it alone. I pray that these daily chapters will bring you close enough to our loving heavenly Father to feel his arms around you and to hear his heartbeat.

After all, God knows full well what it's like to lose a child.

Acknowledgements

I could not have survived the wilderness of miscarriage without the support of my friends and wider family. Even when you thought your contribution was minimal, it helped, believe me. Thank you.

I would like to thank all those who shared the writing process with me:

Mark, for his constant support and for never complaining of neglect when I disappeared for great lengths of time in order to write.

Fiona, Lou, Mandy, Ingrid, Maureen and Kay for taking the trouble to read the unpolished manuscript and offer their invaluable feedback.

My writing group, part of the Association of Christian Writers, who have been the best encouragers anyone could hope for.

Jenny and Tish, two women involved on the front line of baby-loss ministry, for reading the manuscript and endorsing it so heartily.

Tony Collins, whose encouragement was immediate and consistent, and whose attention to detail assured me I was in safe hands.

Jennifer Rees Larcombe, for championing the book when it was still a mere idea and for cheering me on as I crossed the finish line. Thanks, too, for the wonderful Foreword.

Thank you to my family for sharing and shaping my story, especially my sons Phil and Rob – great brothers to each other and, no doubt, to their siblings they will one day meet.

Day 1

My baby was real

———•·•———

If you had just arrived at my door, I would invite you in, give you a hug before you'd had time to wrestle yourself out of your coat, then go through to the kitchen to put the kettle on. As it is, we won't be meeting up in the flesh, but welcome to the equivalent of the comfy chair in my lounge where we'll think about things and probably – actually, certainly – cry together.

I'm sorry you're here, of course, because that means you've lost a baby – maybe more than one baby – and you're desperate to feel better. There will be things we can share, experiences that parallel your own, and there is great comfort to be found in knowing that someone else understands what you're going through. Some of these pages will give information I hope you'll find helpful in going forward; although some questions may never be answered . . .

None of us wanted to join the 1-in-4 club. We are reluctant members, but it is my deepest hope that at least by being together it won't feel quite so terrible. Although we have to go through a lot of this on our own, we don't have to be *alone*, if you understand the difference. This time is for you, to come away from everything else for a while so that you can feel a bit stronger to face 'normal life' again.

Except that nothing feels quite normal any more.

For the rest of the planet it seems it's 'business as usual' but your world has been turned upside down by your miscarriage. You walk down the street and notice that everyone else is getting on with their lives – catching their usual bus, doing the supermarket run, drinking coffee at their favourite place – and wonder how they could, at a time like this. All this happened to me. I went through the motions, watching it in a kind of daze, as if I was peering through glass at a world that had suddenly become closed to me.

Nobody could tell I was screaming inside. From the outside I must have looked the same, although my reflection told me the light had gone from my eyes. My loss had been a private one. Hardly anyone knew that I had been pregnant. My unborn child, whose presence could have changed the world, had slipped away unknown. For most other people, she wasn't even real.

It was my first miscarriage. I didn't know how I was supposed to react. I didn't know how other people would respond when I told them. In church, the Sunday after it had happened, I whispered to the elderly friend next to me, 'I had a miscarriage, Betty.' She simply slipped a bony arm around my shoulders, her eyes glistening. She had lost several of her own, I knew; and no words were necessary. Others were cross with me for not telling them I'd been pregnant. Still others shrugged it away as if it didn't matter; after all, I could always try again.

I've been a Christian most of my life, but not much had happened that had been too difficult to deal with. So, miscarriage was a test of a lot of things, including my relationship with God. Reading the Bible really helped. I found again and again that its words adjusted my thinking as its truths spoke into my deepest recesses. This verse was one that really struck me at the time: 'Why would you ever complain . . . saying "God has lost track of me. He doesn't care what happens to me"? Don't you know anything? Haven't you been listening? God doesn't come and go. God *lasts*' (Isaiah 40.27–28, The Message).

Our precious babies were not overlooked by God. We will never know why they 'didn't make it', and deep down we know that no answer would completely satisfy our hearts anyway. One thing is for sure: our babies were real! We may not have met them, but we loved them from the moment we knew about them. Sometimes, that knowledge arrives too late and we find ourselves loving them in hindsight; but they truly existed.

My second miscarriage was at 13 weeks and a scan showed no heartbeat. Calling the surgical procedure 'removal of the products of conception' was heartless in itself. When it came to the time to be discharged, I had the misfortune to be dealt with by an obviously tired nurse with no sympathy. She explained to me that I had a blighted ovum: a foetus that had failed to develop. It wasn't really a baby and I hadn't really had a miscarriage, she added. I remember looking her fully in the face and saying that we had lost a much longed for baby, not merely a formless cluster of cells. We named her Lydia.

One night, we were talking in bed, and I was going over the painful fact of our baby not having a heartbeat. I was praying inside my head as I spoke and suddenly I broke off with a 'Did you hear that?' I shifted position in the dark, but the sound continued loud in my ears: the unmistakable 'galloping horse' heartbeat of a baby in the womb. I listened in wonder, and as the sound faded and my tears began to flow, I marvelled at the God who wanted to let me know that not only did my baby have a heartbeat, but it was beating still, somewhere beyond my reach but within the grasp of my (and her) heavenly Father.

Response

Loving Father God, thank you for the gift of my child. I'm finding it unbearable that my baby has gone and I'm struggling to continue alone. Thank you that you know my baby's name and that he/she is safe with you. Please help me as I grieve this terrible loss and try to get through it all. Help me trust you more and more.
Amen.

Day 1

_____

_____

_____

_____

_____

_____

_____

_____

_____

_____

_____

_____

_____

_____

Day 2

Stop! I want to get off!

————◆◆◆————

After my third miscarriage, I had been rather low and the depression that had enveloped me after the second one was threatening to return. Some friends had a pair of tickets to Alton Towers which they couldn't make use of, so they offered them to us: would we like a day out, a chance to forget our troubles for a short while? Well, put like that, of course we readily accepted. We didn't admit to them or ourselves that it wasn't really 'our thing'.

The first ride we tried was fairly tame, by all accounts. We managed to survive and I hadn't screamed too much, so we contemplated our next one. Trying to decide, we sat for a while on a bench and watched a ring of pods going round and round horizontally, not far above ground level. That looked safe! We joined the queue and soon found ourselves strapped into a pod, me in front and my husband behind. The ride began, its circuits seeming to speed up, gently at first then gaining momentum; as they did, the ring of pods lifted and continued rising until by the time we reached the top we were actually upside down. I could hardly breathe, and a high-pitched voice behind me said, 'I didn't know it did this!' No indeed. We had watched it come in to land, but we hadn't seen the full cycle. Our expectations were completely skewed.

When we find out we are expecting a baby, we generally have a rosy view of what's to come. We find ourselves drifting off into daydreams of strolling through the park with a pram, our partner and friends looking on in admiration. Not for us any screaming, overtired toddlers in the supermarket! If we allow a peep in our mind's eye to the labour, we imagine a panting woman being wheeled through hospital corridors, disappearing behind a pair of closed doors, only to emerge moments later with a cherub wrapped up in a pink or blue blanket, a contented smile on the faces of all concerned. We have a happy ending resolutely in place.

No one mentions – why would they? – that there may be trouble ahead. And certainly no one breathes a word of the possibility of it all going wrong. The most you may hear is the 'sensible' suggestion that it is best to wait until the 12-week marker before sharing the news, but still no one really talks about why. So, we climb into the roller-coaster cart, looking briefly at the safety warnings at the barrier but telling ourselves it's all going to be such fun!

Except that for you and me, it wasn't. Having strapped ourselves in for this journey of parenthood, we can't seem to get off. All around us people are pregnant and having babies and being happy and there seems no escape. The ride, which felt exciting at the beginning, has turned into a relentless, stomach-churning, head-spinning nightmare.

Now, here's the thing. When you are on a theme park ride, you are belted up tightly inside your carriage or pod. It can shake you round and about, upside down and practically inside out, but you are still strapped in. Those rails may take you on a corkscrew journey but there is a fixed start point and a fixed end. If you hold your nerve, you will get to the finish.

The fact is, we are strapped into a more secure, enveloped type of carriage than we could ever imagine: the arms of God. We might shake and rattle and fear we will fall or be flung off into the distance, but even if we are, we will still be in his arms. He is never going to let go!

> So we will never fear
> even if every structure of support were to crumble away.

6

We will not fear even when the earth quakes and shakes,
moving mountains and casting them into the sea.
For the raging roar of stormy winds and crashing waves
cannot erode our faith in you.

(Psalm 46.2–3, TPT)

Right now, you are part of a process you don't want to be in. With all your heart, you want to 'get off'. Gently, I'm reminding you that you have no choice at the moment. But it will stop, at some point. I can still remember roller-coasters I have been on at Alton Towers and Legoland and have the photo to remind me of how old I looked with my neck muscles taut and my knuckles white as they gripped the handrail. I can look back and remember, and give thanks for the way God has brought me through. Not just silly things like a theme park ride, but the roller-coaster of life itself and specifically miscarriage. God is faithful, you know. I can bear witness to that. I'm not going to pretend it's not horrible. You may feel more pain than you ever believed it was possible to without actually dying. But you will come through, because he who promised is faithful; and I want to remind you of that today. Even when you don't feel you have the strength to keep holding on, he will never let go.

Response

Sit quietly for a moment and try to feel strapped in by arms that surround you in love. Imagine the roller-coaster ride coming in to land as you lean into them. Let your whole system calm down and relax. If you want to pray, thank God for his protection as well as asking for his help.

_____

_____

_____

_____

Day 3

How are you?

On a daily basis, this question is tossed between two people as carelessly as playing frisbee in the park. I've done it many times myself; the words fall out of the mouth so easily. At the moment, there may be times when you're praying for someone to just ask how you are; for someone to show they care, that they remember. Even though you may have said the same things again and again, you're still not done. So, hearing the words 'How are you?' makes your heart sing. You take a deep breath to start, only to realize that, today, they meant nothing more than 'hello'. A look into their eyes confirms that they haven't the time or interest in how you are at all. Behind your smile, your heart feels as if it's died a little bit more.

Let's be honest, it's not even as if you could have answered the question easily anyway. It's like someone asking you to describe the shapes you see in desert sand when a strong wind is blowing: it's constantly changing. You might have felt reasonably OK when you left the house, but the journey to work might have contained any number of things that tipped you over the edge. I remember one time I was sitting watching a crime drama on telly. When the newly pregnant main character went into the ladies', I felt a jolt in my stomach and just knew what was going to happen. Sure enough, she came out of the cubicle saying she was bleeding and the tears began rolling down my face. Oh, I'd been fine when I sat down for the evening, but a simple trigger like that had broken me again.

In the end, I gave up even trying to answer the question and often simply replied, 'Thanks for asking. I appreciate it.' Real friends learned that this meant it wasn't a very good day; and their facial expression and little touch of their hand communicated what words could not. The rest would walk away with a puzzled look.

From the moment I gave my heart to Jesus at the age of seven, I knew I had someone who totally cared about how I was. All right, I didn't exactly hear 'How are you?' being boomed from heaven, but I would open up my Bible and find words that somehow managed to hit the spot. Time and again I feel I have a God who has read my diary, confirming the familiar words of Psalm 139.4: 'Before a word is on my tongue you know it completely, O LORD.'

There may not be many people in your life who have the time to find out how you are. Some know that they wouldn't be able to cope with your honesty. Some have run out of variations of the same phrases. Some will actually believe that you should be over it by now. All of this can fuel your sense of loneliness and sadness. But – and this is the real consolation, not just 'mind over matter' – God knows and he cares. He is not going to turn round and change the subject. He's not going to criticize you when you can't process what's happening. He has endless patience, a bottomless capacity for caring and showing he cares.

I know you want to get out of this place you're in. You didn't ask to be here and every morning you wake up hoping it hasn't really happened. But since the circumstances can't change, the only thing that can become different is you-within-the-circumstances – and you don't even have to do that bit without his help.

There is an open 'How are you?' from God. Every time you think of him or turn your face towards him, the question is there. He wants to hear what you have to say.

Response

Try now just closing your eyes and daring to tell it like it is. Forget the fragments and snippets that your friends are satisfied with. Tell him all of it. His shoulders are broad enough to take it; his ears are always listening. Don't just 'hit and run'. When you've finished saying what you need to, don't rush away. Linger long enough to sense him close to you. You may even hear him speaking . . .

_____

_____

_____

_____

_____

_____

_____

_____

_____

_____

_____

_____

Day 4

Strengthen yourself in the Lord 1

If you're anything like all the other women I know in this situation, you will find that for the most part you are dealing with it all alone. You may well have a loving partner, a set of caring parents and some 'through thick and thin' type of friends. Perhaps only yesterday you managed to have the heart to heart you needed; you had a shoulder you could lean against as you wept. Maybe someone called you, or sent a text that helped you get through the next five minutes. But even if all that support has been yours – and let's be honest, some days are better stocked with kindness than others – there will be those moments when you are alone. The bedside light is off, your partner has started to snore and you feel completely isolated.

Even on an ordinary journey, it is still your own legs that have to keep going up and down! Having companionship really helps morale, but you still have to put in the effort yourself. How much more so on this journey you had no intention of being on. The doctors are there to intervene, but it is *your* body that needs to heal. You can cry with a friend, but you still have to live with *your* aching, breaking heart. You are the one who has to face the world when you'd rather hide. Agony, all of it.

But I believe that, as Christians, we are never alone. When the rest of the world is either sleeping or silent, God is still at his post, never slumbering, never dozing off, and always singing his song of love over you. Linger for a moment over these thoughts: *you are never alone.* I had a friend who in a really difficult season of my life would ring me up a couple of times a week and say repeatedly the words of Jesus, 'I will never leave or forsake you.' There was something in the repetition that worked its way into my soul and I would weep silently on the other end of the line and let the truth do its work. I was physically on my own but emotionally, spiritually, in the depths of my core, I was connected to the Father with unbreakable bonds of love.

In 1 Samuel 30 we read how David was in a hideous situation. He was yet again being pursued by King Saul, who made no secret of the fact he wanted to kill him. He was even living among the enemy for his own safety, but had witnessed his town being attacked and burned, the women and children – including his own – kidnapped. On top of everything, he was being blamed for not stopping it happening. He was at the end of his tether. Verse 4 says, 'So David and his men wept aloud until they had no strength left to weep.' I know that feeling. Don't you? But just a couple of verses later, we read, 'But David found strength in the LORD his God.'

I don't know about you, but I am prone to cynicism. When I hear about blessings or miracles in church, I find it all too easy to say, 'Oh well, it would happen to *them*, wouldn't it?' Some people seem to have all their prayers answered and their problems melt away. Perhaps it's tempting to look at David and think along those lines. We know he is described as a 'man after God's heart' and so of course he was able to strengthen himself in the Lord. After all, why would God withhold strength from his chosen one?

There's a fridge magnet I've seen that says, 'Jesus loves everyone, but I'm his favourite.' I love that! We are all his favourites. Now, I don't know why some people's prayers are answered and other people's are not. But I do know that these words are spoken to everyone who reads them: 'Call to me and I will answer you' (Jeremiah 33.3).

Right now, when you are mourning your lost baby and dealing with the fall-out that goes with that, is the time to do what David did and strengthen yourself in the Lord. Don't wait for the pastor to call round. Don't sit next to a silent phone. Don't tell yourself that you'll feel better when x, y or z happens. Strengthen yourself in the Lord.

How? There will be any number of things that will help you move towards this, but start by sitting quietly in your room. In the silence invite God to come. You may feel him draw close, you may not; but he will come. You want real strength, not a quick fix, so don't rush away. Give yourself time to tell God what you need to say. Tell him you cannot do this on your own; that unless he shows up, you're done for. Consciously do away with your own agenda and simply ask him to come.

Response

Lord, I need you. I need to know that you are here with me in this place. I cannot stand the feelings I have, the pain I'm going through. There's no one who can help me like you can, Jesus. What I'm going through is too much, too heavy. It's crushing me. I believe that you were raised from the dead, that you rolled the stone away. Please roll this burden away from me. Lift me out of the grave and give me strength to live again, to face today and tomorrow.

Strengthen yourself in the Lord 1

_____
_____
_____
_____
_____
_____
_____
_____
_____
_____
_____
_____
_____
_____
_____

Day 5

Strengthen yourself in the Lord 2

———◦•◦———

We can be pretty sure that David found strength in writing the Psalms: those poems of incredible honesty, of 'warts and all' faith, which he could then sing as he went through the day. Have you tried writing a poem or a song? It doesn't have to be of award-winning quality, but it might help to get the feelings out and to offer them to God to deal with. I used to sit at the piano and sing terribly melancholic songs that sometimes depressed me more than they helped me, but I would listen to what was coming out of my mouth and be able to understand myself a bit better. Sometimes you don't really know how you feel until you say it out loud.

Here is one of my songs, written with tears pouring down my cheeks, but managing somehow to give me a poignant smile.

> Cry, whisper a name,
> And we'd be right there, back where we came.
> If we knew then what we do,
> Would life be the same?
> Would anything change?
>
> For then, we were two such different people.
> Then, we could laugh at tragedy.
> For we were children, playing with fire,
> Believing we could be free.

> Thoughts, trapped in the past,
> Can seem to escape, deny being lost.
> We can try all in our power
> But still they are there, still they are there.
>
> For now, we are two such different people.
> Now we've been burned by tragedy.
> No longer children, but still naive,
> Believing we could be free.

There is a wistfulness about these words as I read them. My husband and I had no idea what pain lay ahead of us as we set out to become parents. We had thoughts of baby powder and prams, not of hospitals and procedures. My worry about the pain of delivery became worry that I would not experience it. Goodness, we both grew up sharpish in those times.

Strength from God is literally your life-saver. You cannot go through this alone, and you don't have to. Just before writing this I noticed the house plant I was given a few months ago looking very poorly. One of its flower spikes had keeled right over and some leaves had gone yellow. With me being far from green-fingered, this plant has done well to survive at all, but I did at least know it needed water. I flushed the pot through with a running tap and let it sit in the gathered water for a bit. Already, it is clearly reviving and looking better for its refreshing.

Isn't that what we need? To be refreshed by the Lord? To receive help from heaven and be allowed to sit in it for a while until we can be back on display?

Response

Once more, find a quiet space on your own. It doesn't have to be your usual spot – God can meet you wherever you are. Ask him to drench you with his love. Not just a sprinkle but a pouring out of everything you need. If it's hard to receive, don't worry. Ask again later, or ask for more now. He wants to refresh you right down to your roots.

Day 6

Duvet days

⸻ ◆ ⸻

He will cover you with his feathers,
and under his wings you will find refuge.
(Psalm 91.4)

The writer of Psalm 91 would never have heard of a 'duvet day' but he seems to have described it pretty well. There are days right now when we cannot face the world. Waking up into another day can feel overwhelming. The thought of having to go out and talk to people is too much. We want to stay put in the comfort and sanctuary of our own bed. I know that sometimes we have no choice. We have to get up and see to the needs of other people, and sometimes that prod is a good thing – going somewhere and doing something that gets us out of ourselves for a while. But today might not feel so good. So, if there is no need to push yourself, then please give yourself full permission to rest.

A friend of mine has what she calls her magic blanket. It's a scruffy old thing. Patchworked lovingly by a relative many years ago, it is somewhat threadbare; to put it in the washing machine might be its literal undoing. So, it remains a bit in need of some TLC itself, but it has the most extraordinary ability to offer comfort. Whenever my friend – or one of her friends – is feeling down, she'll reach into the bottom of her wardrobe and bring it out for service.

One of the best comforts for our empty bodies is a good hug. The trouble is, they don't seem to last anything like long enough! When my son was small, if he fell over and hurt himself I used to say to him, 'Just hold on until you feel better.' I would feel his arms tighten around my waist while he sobbed, only releasing their grip once the pain had subsided. If only our pain were as short-lived and easily fixed as a grazed knee! We want someone to hold on to until it feels better, but there aren't many people who have enough time for us. Long after their touch is just a memory we find ourselves craving as much reassurance as when the embrace began. There is something quite unquenchable about that primeval need to be held.

Covered in my friend's shabby blanket, I found that it did have a kind of magic. Its weight on my shoulders was like arms reaching around me and pulling me close. Maybe it was something to do with the act of offering it to me in the first place? There is something wonderfully warming about someone being kind. All I know is that within its folds I found unlikely comfort.

Psalm 91 talks about both comfort and covering.

> You who sit down in the High God's presence,
> spend the night in Shaddai's shadow,
> Say this: 'God, you're my refuge.
> I trust in you and I'm safe!'
> That's right – he rescues you from hidden traps,
> shields you from deadly hazards.
> His huge outstretched arms protect you . . .'
> (Psalm 91.1–13, The Message)

Do you see that image? He is protecting you with arms big enough and wide enough to completely envelop you in the kind of hug that leaves you gasping for air! 'He will cover you with his feathers . . .' like a snuggly down-filled quilt, warming and reassuring, with the Father's arms holding you tightly within it. Your heart is empty and aching but that 'magic blanket' comforts and soothes.

Response

Grab your dressing gown or your duvet – or get yourself into bed – and imagine being surrounded by God's love. He is close to you right now. He is not going to rush away or call time on it. Hold on to him until the pain eases. Let the tears flow. Offer him the pain of your heart. Whether you can speak it out or not, he hears. Whether you can hear him or not, he is singing quietly over you.

_____

_____

_____

_____

_____

_____

_____

_____

_____

_____

_____

_____

_____

Day 7

Psalm 39

Here's my life motto, the truth I live by:
I will guard my ways for all my days.
I will speak only what is right, guarding what I speak.
Like a watchman guards against an attack of the enemy,
I'll guard and muzzle my mouth
When the wicked are around me.
I will remain silent and will not grumble or speak out of
my disappointment.
But the longer I'm silent my pain grows worse!
My heart burned with a fire within me,
and my thoughts eventually boiled over
until they finally came rolling out of my mouth.
'Lord, help me to know how fleeting my time on earth is.
Help me to know how limited is my life
and that I'm only here but for a moment more.
What a brief time you've given me to live!
Compared to you my lifetime is nothing at all!
Nothing more than a puff of air, I'm gone so swiftly.
So too are the grandest of men;
they are nothing but a fleeting shadow!'

Psalm 39

We live our lives like those living in shadows.
All our activities and energies are spent for things that
pass away.
We gather, we hoard, we cling to our things,
only to leave them all behind for who knows who.
And now, God, I'm left with one conclusion:
my only hope is to hope in you alone!

How fleeting and frail our lives!
We're nothing more than a puff of air.

Lord, listen to all my tender cries.
Read my every tear, like liquid words that plead for your
help.
I feel alone at times, like a stranger to you,
passing through this life just like all those before me.
Don't let me die without restoring
joy and gladness to my soul.

(Psalm 39.1–7, 11–13, TPT)

Response

As you read the words of the psalm, skim over the phrases that don't apply to how you are feeling today, and pause at the ones that do. Never be afraid to 'spit out the pips' as you take in the fruit of God's word.

Peace to you, in Jesus' name, today!

23

Day 7

Day 8

The kindness of God

The story of Abraham and Sarah in the book of Genesis, chapters 18, 20 and 21, might be familiar. This dear old couple had reached a very grand age – he was 99 and she was 90 – and had celebrated all the major wedding anniversaries, but had not managed to achieve the thing they most wanted: to be parents. I imagine them attending the baby showers of their friends, then the children of their friends and even the grandchildren of their friends; but no one needed to throw a party for them. Sarah must have thought her chance had well and truly gone.

She came up with a Plan B: offering her maid Hagar to Abraham. I don't blame her for that. After endless years of trying, it was fairly clear that Plan A was not working. She may not have suffered miscarriage but, like us, she certainly knew month after month of nothing happening. When she spent time thinking about the promise God had made to Abraham – about him becoming the father of nations – she might have worked out that it didn't actually mention her being the mother, did it? I can easily see how, in her disappointment and pain, she might have thought that the promise to her husband would come true if she took herself out of the picture. In her head, it made sense to move aside.

What happened next proved to be disastrous. Yes, Abraham did have a son – Ishmael; but far from creating a family, his arrival caused more problems than they could have imagined. And jealousy between Sarah and Hagar was the biggest.

The Bible tells us very little of Sarah's feelings, but we can hazard a good guess. When the angel originally turned up to tell Abraham he was going to become a father, Sarah laughed. This wasn't a carefree laugh; in fact, I'm pretty sure it had very little to do with humour. Sarah was cynical, hurting and mistrustful. I see myself in that description. Do you? But, oh, the kindness of God! To keep choosing her anyway, with no suggestion that she had invalidated the promise; to bless her with her heart's desire long after it had crusted over with disappointment.

Response

How are you today? Will it be a day when you feel your heart lifting in hope, or dropping in despair? Can you cope with what you may have to face? Please be very kind to yourself. Don't expect any more from yourself than you can give. Don't try to drum up false hope or enthusiasm. Don't feel that you have to stick on a false smile. Wherever you go, whatever you do today, can you cling on to the kindness of God? You never have to pass an audition to merit his kindness. He is kind, full stop. Whether you're hurting or healing, God thinks you're amazing!

_____

_____

_____

_____

_____

_____

_____

_____

_____

_____

_____

_____

_____

_____

_____

_____

_____

_____

_____

_____

_____

_____

_____

Day 9

To be honest . . .

And the truth will set you free.
(John 8.32)

There are many times when I feel that it's the truth that gets you into trouble. Confessing as a child that it was you who broke the vase, or the greenhouse window. Telling a friend she looks like a banana in her new yellow outfit when she insisted she wanted to know what you thought.

I'm sure that on most days you probably feel that it's easier to say you're fine rather than go through the rigmarole of trying to explain why you're not. There seem so few who will stop long enough to listen. The things you want to be honest about are so difficult to voice. It's easier to just keep pretending.

I hate lies. I've been lied to too many times in my life, with devastating consequences. I resolved a long time ago not to lie, even if it was a difficult truth. But only recently I realized something I simply had not spotted: that in telling myself things were OK when they weren't, I wasn't exactly lying, but I certainly wasn't being honest. It's much easier for everyone around us if we are OK. So we might as well tell them that we are and not rock the boat, or provoke that discussion, or risk that rejection. Easier all round.

But what happens to our hearts? It can get to the point when we're telling our *soul* we're OK when we're not – lying to the very core of who we are! The thing about the Psalms is their raw honesty. Some people find them difficult

28

because of that: they strip back the pretence and tell it like it is. There's a section of Psalm 139 that is usually bypassed when read in church. 'Away from me, you bloodthirsty men' (verse 19) doesn't sound as cosy as 'Before a word is on my tongue, you know it completely, O LORD' (verse 4).

But isn't that exactly the point? God *does* know what we're thinking. He knows the words we're about to speak and the ones we swallow down. He knows that there are times when anger rages inside us and we want to just lash out. Even when we don't act on those feelings – and most of the time we're self-controlled enough to rein them in – we have to be honest enough to admit to ourselves it's how we're feeling.

When Psalm 42.5 says, 'Why are you downcast, O my soul?' how do you imagine the voice sounding? Is the psalmist angry with his soul for being so fed up? Or is he genuinely wondering what's going on 'in there'? Actually, I think the psalmist knows exactly what's up. He knows the things in life that have happened, and how each thing has made him feel. Just like you do!

One of the benefits of being honest is that it will prevent bitterness from creeping in. If you're not careful, there will be some resentment that finds its place in among the assertions of 'I'm fine'. There will be part of you left screaming silently in the background. Being honest with yourself keeps your heart healthy. Making yourself feel the pain will hurt, unavoidably, I'm afraid; but better that than letting your heart crust over so that you *can't* feel.

If you are honest with your partner or your close friend or family member and they handle your honesty badly, that mustn't stop you being honest. People want you to feel better: genuinely for your sake and selfishly for theirs. Your misery upsets them and they don't want to be upset; but living around other people means that we bear each other's burdens. Your honesty is training for them – if they choose to see it that way. If they respond to your honesty well, then both parties benefit. If they don't – well, yes, you face more pain; but you have been true to yourself, and that's the crucial thing.

Admitting your pain to yourself does not mean you will constantly be feeling the pain. Sometimes we know that to get distracted for a while is wonderful respite: hours might go by without us thinking about 'it'. But constantly telling yourself 'no', not giving yourself permission or opportunity to feel it or think about it, means that you are repressing it: squashing it down. The trouble is, that repressed emotion has an energy of its own. It is like a volcano rumbling away in the depths, ready to burst. Releasing the pain appropriately means that it's dealt with. The tears, the aching throat, the pain in your chest will ease each time. Short-lived necessary release avoids long-term hard-heartedness.

Whatever you are feeling, be honest enough to admit you're feeling it. If there is no one else to listen, God is a constant listening ear. As Psalm 142.2 says, 'pour out' your complaint to God. Really! Do it! Get that roar heard! When the emotions are spent, the tears still wet on your cheeks, your breath still rasping, listen to your heart. There will be a peace there that he has dropped in. From somewhere deep within, there will be a sense of your voice saying, 'It is well with my soul.' Whether it lasts for 30 seconds, or hours or days, enjoy it. There will always be peace after a battle. Just decide that you are no longer going to fight with yourself. You are not going to tell yourself it is different from what it is. Be honest, be real. And the truth will set you free.

Response

Take some paper and write down the things that have made your soul downcast. This is not for you to show to anyone else, so be honest. If you have been putting on a brave face – even to yourself – this is your moment to admit the pain, or disappointment, or anger, or whatever. There's no one here to contradict you, or suggest that you are wrong for how you feel. If you don't feel you're coping, write it down. You will be spending the vast majority of your time trying to carry on as normal. You may fool others, and maybe even yourself, but please be honest enough to admit that sometimes you can't.

To be honest . . .

Sometimes you haven't got the physical and emotional energy. It would be wonderful if it could be different, but for now, it is how it is.

_____

_____

_____

_____

_____

_____

_____

_____

_____

_____

_____

_____

Day 10

The rescue mission

I waited and waited and waited some more,
patiently, knowing God would come through for me.
Then, at last, he bent down and listened to my cry.
He stooped down to lift me out of danger
from the desolate pit I was in,
out of the muddy mess I had fallen into.
Now he's lifted me up into a firm, secure place
and steadied me while I walk along his ascending path.

(Psalm 40.1–2, TPT)

It was winter, not many weeks short of Christmas, and I had escaped to a retreat centre in the south of England for a few days away. I went alone, and knew no one when I got there. I kept my head down and my conversations brief; but I listened, and hoped God would meet me.

One morning, as I came to from sleep, I could see a triangle of yellow light in my dream. I was awake enough to be curious, and in my mind's eye followed the light to see what it was. As it came better into view, so to speak, I realized that it was the beam of a torch, coming closer towards me the more I looked. My heartbeat quickened – because I recognized that the holder of the torch was on a rescue mission to find me in the darkness of my desolation. If I hadn't realized it before, I now knew with certainty that I had got myself into a very dark place and couldn't find my own way out.

In the evening meeting, later that same day, the retreat leaders were reading out some Bible verses they felt might be relevant to those of us gathered there. The psalm quoted above was referred to, along with a picture of a ladder reaching into a deep pit. Far from being comforted, I felt angry. I took that picture to mean that I had to do all the hard work. I was the one who had to climb every steep rung to get to the surface, when I had no energy to do anything but stay on the floor of the pit.

One of the leaders came up to me once the meeting was over. She wondered if I had found any of it helpful. I shook my head in misery. I felt worse, if anything. When I told her that it was cruel to make me fight my own way out of the pit, she struggled to believe I had taken it so negatively. 'That's not it at all! Jesus puts the ladder down into the pit, then climbs down it himself, ready to carry you up to safety.'

Oh! Of course! I had visions, then, of being rescued: carried over the shoulder, fireman-style. No hero would just lean the ladder against the side and walk away. He would want the satisfaction of knowing the trapped person was safe.

Don't our thoughts become so tangled and distorted when we're 'in the pit'? We can't see our own hand in front of our face. We are tired, bruised from the fall, alone and helpless. I expect you've tried your best to dust yourself off and start again but it's an almost impossible task. Whenever I felt I was getting somewhere, the entrance to the pit would still seem dangerously close. One careless word from someone could push me back in. When we're hurting so much following a miscarriage, we really haven't the strength to get ourselves out; but God never intended that we should.

Psalm 40 says that God stoops down to lift us out of danger. We don't have to reach up. He reaches down. What's more, he doesn't just drop us by the edge, out of the pit but still in harm's way. He puts us down in a firm, secure place and even holds our hand while we regain our balance.

Response

Today, if you're tired and feel you have no fight left; if you're desperate to get out from where you've fallen but can't manage to climb up the sides; call out to God to come and rescue you. The way he does it may take you by surprise. It may not happen immediately. But there is no way that he is planning to abandon you. For all you know, the rescue mission has been launched and is already on its way. Soon, you can be out of the darkness and held safely within his loving arms.

_____

_____

_____

_____

_____

_____

_____

_____

_____

_____

_____

_____

_____

Day 11

Mornings of joy

If you've ever sung the old hymn 'O worship the Lord in the beauty of holiness', you'll recognize these lines from verse four: 'Mornings of joy give for evenings of tearfulness; trust for our trembling and hope for our fear'. More recently in church we've been singing 'Your love never fails', which says, 'There may be pain in the night but joy comes in the morning.'

'But joy . . .'

I expect you've had many evenings of tearfulness lately. Even when I'd been crying on and off during the day, I felt no less emotional when it was over. It didn't seem to matter whether it had been a good day or a bad one; once evening came, the tears would start again. I would go to bed exhausted, 'all cried out'.

I would be lying if I said I always woke up from one of my 'crying myself to sleep' nights feeling refreshed and ready to face the day; but there is a curious kind of peace that comes from having had a good cry. It might be too much of a stretch to call it 'joy' but you can be aware of a pause, some respite from the grief, that you are only too grateful for.

Interestingly, a 2008 study in the USA into the effects of crying found that most people felt less stressed after they'd had a good cry.* However anxious they had been before – and even during – crying, the relief felt afterwards

---

* 'Cry Me a River: The Psychology of Crying', *Science Daily*, 19 December 2008.

more than made up for it. What is more, when a person was comforted while they cried, the relief benefits were magnified.

As well as helping to release the pressure, crying can act as a bridge between you and others. Only the most hard-hearted can stand back and watch someone cry without at least offering a tissue or a little touch to the shoulder. This gesture of connection may be all you need to break down the loneliness and emptiness, and it will fill you, as if you're plugged into the power supply.

Why does God promise joy in the morning? Well, he's been your comforter all through the night as you've slept (or not slept . . .). He has been singing songs of love over you the whole time. And this is the best bit for me: he says that there are new mercies to be had every single day. The moment you wake up, you have access to fresh reserves. You don't have to gee yourself up, get yourself going, push yourself forward. No. It will be as if someone has put you on charge while you slept and now you're awake you feel – against the odds – that you're able to face the new day you were dreading.

This isn't a one-time process, and fortunately it's not a one-time deal either! You may cry yourself to sleep every night for a while, but God is the one who never sleeps and he keeps watch over you.

Response

Let the tears fall. Do not hold them back like you've had to all day. Cry on your own if that gives you the privacy you need, but let others around you comfort you if they are there. Imagine that 'magic blanket' of God's comfort as an arm around your shoulders. When you've finished, take deep breaths and only re-enter the world when you're completely ready. Rest is a really good idea right now . . .

_____

_____

_____

_____

_____

_____

_____

_____

_____

_____

_____

_____

_____

_____

Day 12

No fear

━━━●◆●━━━

Whether you're usually a glass half-empty or glass half-full sort of person, I expect you're finding that life feels all a bit negative. In 'normal' circumstances, things like worry, pain and fear are short-lived. They are triggered by fairly routine stresses that will settle once the event has passed. They come and go and we cope fairly well with that. After miscarriage, however, it feels like one of those disaster movies where the cable car has been shaken from its mountings and is left dangling precariously over the valley. All it would take is a sudden gust or impact to send it plummeting.

Following the trauma of miscarriage, negative emotions such as fear seem to have taken up permanent residence, and before you know it you are fearful and worried about things that normally wouldn't bother you at all. Note that I've used the word 'trauma'. The word is defined in the dictionary as 'injury, or emotional and psychological damage'. We think of a terrible wound on the body as a trauma. It is no exaggeration to apply this word to the experience of miscarriage, where the loss of our baby – sometimes made much worse by the actual physical process – leaves us sucker-punched and literally bleeding. The psychological condition of post-traumatic stress disorder (PTSD) is now commonly recognized; but it might not be quite so readily understood that a woman who has miscarried may end up suffering from it.

Being afraid, like some of the other negative things you are feeling, is normal for now. The problem with fear is that it acts as a magnifying glass for lots of other things. Everything we see and feel at the moment is filtered through the lens of fear. Things that were easy for us, like socializing and going to work and existing contentedly within our bodies, are suddenly difficult. We fear bumping into someone – especially a pregnant someone; we dread the unexpected or unwelcome conversation; we don't trust our body or our emotions. We fear breaking down in public. You may even have had a panic attack or something that felt close to it.

In my case, I found that fear made me overthink terribly. After my second miscarriage, whereas looking back I can see I was suffering from depression, I got it into my head that I had pelvic inflammatory disease. I was terrified I wouldn't be able to conceive again because of the damage PID was doing 'down there'. I went to my GP, who dismissed my concerns so peremptorily that I left his surgery in tears. I needed reassurance and got only his impatience.

You are probably afraid of what you're turning into. Several women have told me that they didn't feel the same person any more and they worried that they would stay like it. You may worry that you won't be able to continue in your job, or still be part of an organization you belong to. You fear you will break down in an important meeting or at the checkout or in the school playground. You can no longer rely on yourself to behave properly and that makes you feel very out of control.

Mostly, I think you'll be afraid about your chances of having another baby. No one can reassure you, I'm sorry to say. Each person is unique, so looking at statistics is no help. When I was scared I was going to lose my first baby, my mum tried to reassure me by saying there was no history of miscarriage in our family. Well, I soon went on to bust that particular record! Considering that for the most part doctors don't know the cause of miscarriage, they are unable to predict with any certainty what may happen in the future. So we end up dealing in chances: there's a three in four chance we'll have a successful pregnancy; but however much we want to pin things down and have things planned, we are unable to control our world.

This is where I remind myself that I know the one who really is in control! Nowhere in the Bible does it promise that things will be rosy; but how about this verse for starters? 'In this world you will have trouble. But take heart! I have overcome the world' (John 16.33).

Response

Spend some time reading through these verses. Not all of them will hit the spot – these things are different for everyone – but if a phrase or two touches your heart, linger over the words and let peace come.

> In the day that I'm afraid, I lay all my fears before you
> and trust in you with all my heart.
>
> (Psalm 56.3, TPT)

> God is a safe place to hide,
> ready to help when we need him.
> We stand fearless at the cliff-edge of doom,
> courageous in seastorm and earthquake.
> (Psalm 46.1, The Message)

> Do not be afraid of them; the LORD your God himself will fight for you.
>
> (Deuteronomy 3.22)

> [Jesus] said to them, 'It is I; don't be afraid.'
> (John 6.20)

Perhaps this old Sunday school song could be your prayer for today:

> I know who holds the future
> And He'll guide me with His hand.
> With God, things don't just happen,
> Everything by Him is planned.

So, as I face tomorrow,
With its problems large and small,
I'll trust the God of miracles,
Give to Him my all.

Day 13

Questions, questions

In the first few hours and days after miscarriage, I felt numb. My body ached, my heart was heavy, my brain was mush; but it didn't take long for my mind to go into hyper-drive. It would start in the middle of the night, when my body craved sleep but none came. *Questions.* Question after question scrolling through my mind as if I was sitting an exam I had no chance of passing.

Why did I lose my baby?
Did I do something wrong?
Why did I miscarry when that other person didn't?
What's wrong with me?
Will it happen again?

Some of these questions would be best aimed at your doctor or gynaecologist, when you get the chance. Officially there are many reasons, and none, for miscarriage. You may well have found out that doctors aren't willing to do any testing or investigation until there have been three miscarriages. Up until that point, they seem to put it down to 'one of those things', which of course is no answer at all. Sometimes testing reveals a reason, and then there is hope of treatment; but sometimes there just doesn't seem to be one definitive cause.

Be reassured, it is very unlikely that you did anything to cause the miscarriage yourself. I blamed myself for the first one because the day before it happened I'd been doing some heavy gardening, and I wondered if I'd over-done it. I know I made everything worse for myself by telling myself I'd been stupid. Please hear me on this: don't beat yourself up. The situation is tough enough without you taking all the responsibility for it.

If you change the emphasis in the question, to 'Why did *I* lose my baby?', then you are maybe asking, 'What's wrong with my body?' Again, this is for the doctors to try to answer. If you are asking, 'Why me, and not them?', well, that's one of those horrible mysteries to which there may never be an answer. Given the statistics, it could have been anyone. It just hurts so much that it was us.

As well as wanting to know the biological reasons for my miscarriages, so that I could stop any more happening, I was trying to make sense of it within my relationship with God. Would you think it odd if I said I've found that some of life's problems are worse because of my faith? Let me quickly explain! Since we believe in a completely loving, sovereign, all-powerful God who loves us with an unshakable love, how do I make that sit alongside what has just happened? If God is the bringer of life and loves me like no one else can, how could he take my baby and make me so unhappy?

I don't know the simple answer to that one, but I started asking whether he was trying to teach me a lesson. If so, how could I learn it quickly so that I could leave this hideousness behind me and walk into glorious motherhood? Was I indulging in sin? Was there something in my family line, some besetting sin from a previous generation, that was affecting me? Was it anything con-nected with an object I owned that was giving off spiritual vibes that caused miscarriage? I actually got rid of my entire collection of Agatha Christie books in case there was a 'spirit of death' connected with them. I repeatedly tied myself in knots trying to work out 'why'.

A song I wrote around that time includes this line: 'Maybe I don't have all the answers, but I'm raising the questions.' There's a certain freedom, a peace, that comes from that statement. I'm saying that it's all right that I don't have all the answers. Before I realized that, I felt I was going mad with trying to work it all out in my head. Sometimes we just have to surrender, to let go. You may not be able to switch off your mind, but you can choose to settle your heart.

How? Well, it's another time to strengthen yourself in the Lord.

Response

As you sit quietly, think of the questions you've been asking recently. Write them down if you like. As you look through them, try to believe that God has the answers even when no one else does. Be honest about how everything is making you feel right now. If you can, keep believing that God is good, and promises to only give good gifts to his children. If that is difficult, then be honest about that, too.

Use the words of this psalm as your prayer for today:

> Look upon all my misery and come be my hero to rescue me,
> for I will never forget what you've revealed to me.
> Take my side and defend me in these sufferings;
> redeem me and revive me, just like you promised you would.
> Your tender mercies are what I need, O God;
> give me back my life again
> through the revelation of your judgments!
> Lord, see how much I truly love your instructions.
> So in your tender kindness, breathe life into me again.
> The sum total of all your words adds up to absolute truth,
> and every one of your righteous decrees is everlasting.
>
> (Psalm 119.153–154, 156, 159–160, TPT)

Amen.

Questions, questions

Day 14

Psalm 41

God always blesses those who are kind to the poor and helpless.
They're the first ones God helps
when they find themselves in any trouble.
The Lord will preserve and protect them.
They'll be honored and esteemed
while their enemies are defeated.
When they are sick, God will restore them,
lying upon their bed of suffering.
He will raise them up again and restore them back to health.
So in my sickness I say to you,
'Lord, be my kind healer.
Heal my body and soul; heal me, God!
For I have confessed my sins to you.'
But those who hate me wish the worst for me, saying,
'When will he die and be forgotten?'
And when these 'friends' come to visit me
with their pious sympathy and their hollow words
and with hypocrisy hidden in their hearts,
I can see through it all.
For they come merely to gather gossip about me,
using all they find to mock me with malicious hearts of slander.
They are wicked whisperers who imagine the worst for me,
repeating their rumors, saying,

'He got what he deserved; it's all over for him!
The spirit of infirmity is upon him and
he'll never get over this illness.'
Even my ally, my friend, has turned against me.
He was the one I totally trusted with my life,
sharing supper with him,
and now he shows me nothing but betrayal and treachery.
He has sold me as an enemy.
So Lord, please don't desert me when I need you!
Give me grace and get me back on my feet
so I can triumph over them all.
Then I'll know you're pleased with me
when you allow me to taste of victory over all my foes.
Now stand up for me and don't let me fall,
for I've walked with integrity.
Keep me before your face forever.
Everyone praise the Lord God of Israel, always and forever!
For he is from eternity past
and will remain for the eternity to come.
That's the way it will be forever.
Faithful is our King! Amen!

(TPT)

Response

_____

_____

_____

_____

_____

_____

Day 14

Day 15

Have a day off!

We're halfway through this month-long journey – high time we had a rest!

You have been focused on becoming a mother for longer than you can remember. Those months of thinking about whether it was time to start a family, or to expand it; then months of trying to conceive; then the weeks following, which brought you to where you are right now. It's been relentless, and quite rightly you deserve a break.

So, I'm suggesting that you have a day off. It might be today: right this minute; DO IT! Or it might need some planning to make the space for it. I'm guessing that it's been a long time since you felt like you used to. You may not even remember what life used to feel like; but today – or whenever you schedule it in – you are going to reconnect with some of the things you used to love before life got so horrible.

It might be that you do this alone – that's perfectly fine if it's the option that fills you with the most anticipation. You may want to share this time with your partner, your best friend, your mum, your sister. What has to be clear is that this day is all about you and what you need. Do not choose a companion who is going to bring you down, make it about them, or in any other way spoil it.

What you do is totally up to you. Shopping, walking in the forest, paddling at the seashore, having afternoon tea at a stately home or a spa day at a hotel. If you let yourself daydream a little, there will be an idea that's just tickling around your mind. It doesn't matter whether it's a sensible suggestion or a crazy one: that's just the point. If you were wondering why I hadn't included white-water rafting in my list, well, that's kind of your answer, isn't it!

The most important thing is that you choose something, someone and somewhere that gives you some respite from your current situation.

No one can keep going indefinitely under extreme stress. Seriously, metaphorically put your feet up. It's when you think you can keep on going that you actually need to stop. So, even if you've been doing well lately and think you can skip this bit: don't.

Have a wonderful day.

See you tomorrow.

_____

_____

_____

_____

_____

_____

_____

_____

_____

_____

_____

_____

_____

Day 16

Time

———◆———

I'm glad you've found a few moments to yourself to read this, because I want to think today about the whole issue of time. We all know that we're not in control of time. It ticks away whether we want it to or not, but there's something more insistent about it now. Lying awake at night, each hour seems twice as long as normal. Waiting for medical appointments to come through feels like an eternity. It's as if the clocks don't work properly any more. And during this season of miscarriage, we notice each month that goes by as well. If we're trying to conceive, then the countdown to the next period is all we're aware of. When it comes, not only do we face the disappointment of not becoming pregnant (or even the fear that we might be) but we grieve all over again because we should still be pregnant.

There was a sense for me, too, that time was running out. Seeing my son grow up, having yet another birthday without him becoming a 'big brother', was excruciating. Friends around me were on their second or third baby. I had never wanted my son to be an only child. My dreams were turning to dust and there was nothing I could do about it. I wonder if, like there was for me, there is an element of panic in your journey right now. It seemed that everyone around me was pregnant; time was passing and I felt that the whole thing would pass me by. Perhaps for you it's your own birthdays that are putting on the pressure?

I do know this much, though: that God is beyond time. He existed before our calendars began and he will continue to exist long after the last page has been flipped over. He doesn't operate within time like we do. He doesn't even measure it the way we do: 'With the Lord a day is like a thousand years and a thousand years are like a day' (2 Peter 3.8). He always keeps his appointments, but sometimes hasn't written them in the diary for us to follow.

A delay doesn't seem to trouble him because for him there is no such thing as delay. His timing is perfect. He doesn't panic or think he's running out of time because it is an endless commodity for him. There's always plenty of time for a little detour on the way to the final destination and you still won't end up being late.

I know – but don't quite understand how – God can also redeem the time. He can restore what has been stolen from us, and repeat opportunities that we may have missed the first or second time around. It says in Joel 2.25, 'I will repay you for the years the locusts have eaten.' He can overwrite whole periods of time.

'Hour by hour I place my days in your hand' (Psalm 31.15, The Message). When I first found this verse in the Bible, I remember looking at it, almost shocked. I had such a sense that this was what I should do from now on. When we live completely ruled by the clock and the schedule of the world, sometimes we need to stand back from it all and breathe in the peace that comes from looking at the world God's way, with his eternal perspective.

You see, our world view of time can really hem us in. We see it as a straight line, a kind of conveyor belt that starts when we are born and continues on until we die. Things that happen are notched into it as we move along. A momentous event disappears into the past along with every other mundane one, while we constantly edge into the future.

It was incredibly painful, following miscarriage, to feel that I was moving further away from where my babies had been in my life. It felt like leaving port on a ferry, me on the deck waving frantically at the one still at the harbourside, until we were out of sight of each other. Time was carrying me forward, when all I wanted was to be able to stay 'back there' with my little one.

But how about looking at it slightly differently? I believe that my children who were born too early in my past are positioned up ahead, waiting to greet me when I finally make it to heaven myself. So, I'm actually edging closer and closer to the time I will be with them for ever. Isn't that a glorious thought? Instead of imagining my ferry leaving port, with my little one left on the quay, I think of it as pressing on to the next port where I will be greeted by a little hand waving a banner to welcome me in!

How about if right now your precious little one is asking, 'Is she here yet?'

Time may not always seem to be 'on our side', but with God's perspective, maybe it doesn't have to be such an enemy.

Response

Turn the clock-face away from you and slip your wristwatch into a drawer. Take a moment with your eternal God to slip into his pulse. Let the stresses dissipate as you consciously focus on our eternal God. Our times are in his hands. Surrender your plans, your schedule, the timings that felt right for you but actually you had no control over.

Imagine being buoyed by the current, resting on the waters, rising and falling in the gentle swell of the waves. You will not go under, or be submerged, but will float safely on the top.

_____

_____

_____

_____

_____

Day 17

In the secret place

———◆◆◆———

We live in a world where everybody's life is laid wide open for all to see. Our friends recount their days in tiny detail during hourly updates on Facebook. Photos on those posts show smiley faces, crowds gathered together. 'Hey! Look at my life!'

But it can't be just me who thinks that what happens in the secret place is of the most value.

Until recently, your baby was growing in the secret, hidden place that Psalm 139 describes so well. You couldn't see him or her developing, but in your mind's eye you had the perfect image of your baby and your future together. You weren't supposed to see your baby so soon. Perhaps you didn't see it at all, but the horrors of passing still occurred. You are right to feel very deeply and strongly about that.

Part of your grieving process will be to let it all out. You will cry and scream and want to talk about it for hours on end. That hidden stuff needs its outlet. But there will come moments – you won't even notice them at first – when God calls you to meet him in the secret place.

What grows in secret places? If conditions are dark, damp, uncared for, then fungus, mould and decay will thrive. Even expensive fungi such as truffles grow in decaying soil. If we don't let light and ventilation into our situation, there is a real danger that we will harbour decay. We don't want our souls to be places of death and stench, but of life and growth.

Let's think of what else can grow in secret places. How about precious gemstones? Formed over thousands of years by pressure within the ground, they are among the most highly prized things on the planet. A pearl, hidden within the shell of the oyster, began as an irritating grain of sand. So, the secret place needn't be a place of stagnation or rot. It can be the very place where the most wonderful thing of your life can happen. I know you wanted that to be your baby, but for now it can't be. You had no choice about that, but you do have a choice as to whether you let God in or not.

If you're anything like me, you will have resisted his invitation on more than one occasion. I couldn't bear to face the openness of my heart that would have to follow. I spent all my time with a brave face on. How could I possibly cope if the mask was taken off?

Eventually, I worked out that God is the only safe place to go. It's confusing because actually he's the one who allowed our child to die. We shouldn't be surprised if that is difficult to process. It takes time to work our way through that one. But I can honestly say that I have always found him to be the only real source of comfort. However painful it is, our souls need the rest that can only be found in the secret place with God. Here is where you can let your guard down, tell him what no one else can bear to hear. And only here is where you can hear his words, which hit the spot like no others.

Response

> My soul thirsts, pants, and longs for the Living God.
> I want to come and see the face of God.
> Day and night my tears keep falling
> and my heart keeps crying for your help.
>
> (Psalm 42.2–3, TPT)

Father, you alone see into the secret place of my heart. I'm not always strong enough to face it, but I want this darkness to produce treasure and not decay. Please come in, and when you do, tread gently. I'm feeling so tender, so raw. I can't bear anything else right now, but I do need you near.

Thank you.

Amen.

_____

_____

_____

_____

_____

_____

_____

_____

_____

_____

_____

_____

_____

Day 18

Turning the water off

In the days, weeks and months after a miscarriage I thought the tears would never stop. How could the human body produce so many tears? I never left the house without a pack of tissues, and indoors there were boxes of them next to every place I sat. The constant crying exhausted me.

In one particular 'monsoon season', it wasn't just my tears that were making everything wet. I noticed a puddle seeping up through the hallway carpet and traced its source to a leaking stop-tap in the airing cupboard. Soon after that, I had problems with the main stopcock outside the front gate. I had the water company on speed-dial! I felt surrounded by water, coming from within me and from the outside. I prayed, my head hanging in despair, and then I heard a quiet voice whispering to my heart, 'I know how to turn the water off.'

I remember sitting bolt upright. Change was coming. I heard it and felt it. Within days all the plumbing problems in the house were sorted and my tears had reduced to a manageable level. I had passed into a normal wet autumn after the torrential summer. The peace of those days was palpable and precious. The intensity of the grief had shifted at hearing that voice.

There's a great story in the Gospels of how Jesus and some of his disciples went on a boat trip. They planned to cross Lake Galilee, as they did often – for them I imagine it was not much different from us popping to town on the bus. The weather was set fair and all was well until a sudden storm overtook them. Storms were commonplace in the region, but this was a bad one. While the disciples fought to retain control of the boat, Jesus was fast asleep. What? On every level, how *could* he? They woke him up, accusing him of not caring that they might drown.

You know, that's quite an accusation. Right now, you may feel as if you're drowning. All it would take is one more wave to knock you right off your feet. And where's Jesus? Gone to sleep on you? It may feel like that. But, you see, Jesus was asleep on the boat because there was nothing to worry about from his perspective. While the disciples were feeling dangerously out of control, Jesus was quietly in charge. They didn't know this yet; but they were about to have their eyes opened. With few words and no shouting, the storm was stilled. The wind and waves responded to the command of the Lord.

Oh, I continued to cry of course. There were still those moments when I'd remember or see something during the day that brought the pain back for a while. As the old song says, there's always something there to remind you. But I felt I now had a companion I could count on. Friends and colleagues were great, up to a point, but their compassion felt only on the surface sometimes. Jesus was the one who took my pain all the way through to the inside. He saw the depth of pain and went down in there for me, turning the water off and stabilizing my system. How could I ever have done any of it without him?

Response

Jesus, you made the storm stop for your disciples on the lake, and I need you to do the same for me now. I know that I need to cry, but I need to be able to stop sometimes. Please speak words over me that will give me peace.
Thank you.
Amen.

Day 18

Day 19

Stormy weather

One of the recognized phases of the grief process is anger. It doesn't really matter where it comes in the sequence, because you will find that anger can bubble up out of nowhere. Just as in various parts of the world there are regions prone to certain weather systems, grief is a place where anger is part of the natural climate.

Do you hear that? Anger is normal, expected and necessary. To deny it would be like saying that the Arctic is no longer cold or that the Sahara is renowned for its bogginess. The trouble is that most Christians have a misunderstanding of anger, believing that we should always be calm, well-mannered and never even lose our cool, let alone feel angry. Would it comfort – or surprise – you to know that the Bible refers to anger 272 times, and most of those references are to God's anger? Famously, Jesus 'lost it' in the Temple where he overturned the tables used by money-lenders exploiting the poor. Why? Because God hates injustice and is right to feel angered by it.

Isn't losing a baby a massive injustice? And that's just for starters. What else do you find yourself (rightfully) angry about?

My baby just died.
I didn't get a chance to make my baby better, my baby just left.
My friend/sister/work colleague got pregnant.
I tried to tell someone how I felt but they looked at me as if I was mad.

> The credit card bill just came in for all the baby stuff I bought that I won't need now.
>
> I'm not pregnant any more and I should be.
>
> That woman in the café can't even control her kids. I would have been a brilliant mum.
>
> I should be a mum.
>
> God let my baby die when he could have stopped it.
>
> My partner doesn't understand me.

Actually, the list goes on and on. Every day brings fresh salt to rub into our wounds, and along with the pain we find ourselves feeling angry. Please do not feel guilty about that! You know that in another season of your life you would be able to walk away without reacting, but this is stormy season and anger is one of the elements. Take a moment to let that sink in. You have a right to be angry. What happened was a bad thing.

The trouble with anger is that it is awful to be on the other end of it. Anyone brought up by an angry parent or taught by an angry teacher knows well the feelings of fear and insecurity caused by their outbursts. When your anger bubbles up, as you know it will, be prepared for it. You wouldn't go out in a rainstorm without a coat or umbrella, so at the moment live as if an emotional storm could brew at any moment. The Bible urges us, 'In your anger do not sin,' so when the red mist forms, try to get away on your own if you possibly can. Don't punch the wall or kick the cat, but grab a pillow and scream into it as loudly as you need to. Or how about directing all that energy that comes with anger towards running fast on the spot? Imagine yourself running away from it all. The beauty of this trick is that exercise releases endorphins, which will increase the sense of peace once the storm has passed.

Try not to take it out on those around you. Even when they're directly to blame, perhaps if they've responded badly when you've tried to open up about your pain, save the anger for when they've gone. You know that however inadequate some of your friends and family are right now, they are literally all you've got. You don't want to drive them away.

The anger will pass, so there will be plenty of chances to spend time with them when you're calmer. If necessary, explain that you're starting to feel angry and either go away yourself or ask them if they wouldn't mind leaving. I gave myself the nickname MOG, which stood for miserable old git, and I would say, 'You'd better go now, MOG's here.' Once the door had closed I could shout and swear and stamp across my bedroom before once more crying my eyes out; but at least I could call my friends later without needing to apologize.

In time, you may find your anger driving you towards a practical outlet. Many a crusade or protest movement has been started by someone who felt angry enough about an issue to do something about it. Harness the feelings! If you have been treated badly by the medical profession, there may be an opportunity at some point to make a formal complaint so that another woman is spared suffering in the future. Some women create jewellery to commemorate lost babies and honour their mothers. Some have written down their stories. Some have formed groups and associations. Some have created a memorial garden (or been a part of an existing one), finding the hard work of digging more than rewarded when the plants came up later. In other words, they have channelled their grief and anger into something positive for themselves and helpful for others.

In my experience, the word that consistently 'calms the storm' is *forgiveness.* Use your periods of anger to identify what you're angry about. Listen to what pours out of your mouth as you rage. Then, while you can still remember, consciously take it to God. Tell him – in whatever words you choose – what you have a problem with. Tell him about how you blame the doctors, or yourself or whoever. Then take a big breath and speak out forgiveness.

Do you know that forgiveness isn't a feeling? In other words, there's no point waiting until you feel like forgiving. When you need to forgive, the only feelings you have are to do with the offence: strong, negative ones. There will be an inner struggle. In your heart, you know you should forgive, but your emotions are likely to fight against it. Think to yourself: 'Do I always want to feel angry like this?' I can't imagine you do. The only way you can get rid of the anger completely is to remove it at source. (Please note, I'm talking specifically about anger and not the grief process as a whole.) When you don't forgive, it's like drinking poison but expecting the person you're angry at to die. That poison is eating you up. It needs to go.

Response

Don't rush. This needs to be genuine. In my experience, once I have started to speak out forgiveness, it's not long before my heart catches up. After a few false starts, I find I really do want to forgive, properly, from my heart.

Dear Jesus, thank you for the offer of forgiveness. Thank you that you have never failed to forgive me. I'm sorry for blaming other people and myself for my baby dying. I'm sorry for blaming you. I don't want to be angry any more, so in Jesus' name I forgive _____ for _____ against me. I forgive myself for taking the blame for things I couldn't control. I surrender my anger to you, Lord, and ask that you keep speaking peace into my storm.
In Jesus' name,
Amen.

_____

_____

_____

_____

_____

_____

_____

_____

Stormy weather

_____
_____
_____
_____
_____
_____
_____
_____
_____
_____
_____
_____
_____
_____

Day 20

The green-eyed monster

I'm not normally the jealous type. All right, at one stage I struggled when I knew how much more than me other people were earning, or I saw the size of their houses compared to mine. As I grew up, though, I suppose I learned contentment, and to trust that God's plan for my life was the perfect fit. But, goodness me, jealousy following miscarriage became a powerful emotional force. Let's be honest, we're not at our best at the moment anyway. It's not a time when we can be reasonable, or satisfied, or sometimes even plain nice. In our acute pain at what we've lost, it's so, *so* hard to look at others without wishing that we had what they have: a baby.

For me, I was jealous not just about the baby but about the size of other people's families. I was resentful that they had planned for their babies to be born at a particular time and it had worked out for them. I saw their children neatly produced in order, the notches on the doorpost all evenly spaced as they grew, and I looked at my one son and felt horribly inadequate. I hated the fact that his friends all had baby brothers or sisters. Those who didn't know I'd miscarried would make crass comments at mother and toddler group, and later in the playground, like 'wasn't it time I had another one?' It was all I could do not to punch them on the nose. Sarcasm was my weapon of choice, but it wasn't an effective one.

I was jealous of the teenagers who got 'knocked up' by accident, maybe not even knowing the father's name, while my husband and I were feeling the strain. How come everyone in the world was pregnant? Wasn't I a good enough mother to my son? Was I being judged as unworthy to become a mother to someone else? Was I so terrible that God couldn't risk me stuffing up someone's life? I honestly felt those things. Not just jealousy coming out there, but guilt and shame and plain raw anger – mostly turned towards myself.

I think the reason for me admitting these things to you is that I want you to know that it's normal. Not a very nice normal, and not your 'normal' normal, but part of the normal that exists for you at the moment. I know that you will try to be self-controlled, and you won't assault people in the street; but you might go home and scream at life's unfairness. And that's OK – because life is unfair, at least from the angle we view it. How come girls who never wanted a baby get to have twins? How come, how come? The answers are not there; it just feels so horribly unfair and we can't do anything about it.

When my sister became pregnant after my fourth miscarriage, I didn't deal with it well. I didn't dare be honest with her about my feelings, and she told me she read the expression on my face as contempt and even disgust. Actually, it was just that I couldn't bear to see her pregnant; I couldn't accept that it was happening to her when it wasn't happening for me. Her daughter was going to be not quite three when her baby number two was due – just the timetable we had been working to in our own family. But now my son was nudging five, and I felt a total failure. I wish we could have had the conversation back then that we needed to. It would have been excruciating, I don't doubt, but not tackling things at the time can cause more pain later if we're not careful.

I was jealous of the ladies known to me whose pregnancies had been threatened but survived. A few days' bed-rest and all was wonderfully well. I felt a failure for that. I felt that I was the only one who had ever miscarried. From my perspective, everyone else had it easy.

How should we deal with jealousy? First, by acknowledging it. Denied feelings always take on a life force of their own. Much better to say it out loud in the privacy of your own space. Don't confess it to the other person – not yet. They are quite likely to say something else that will make you feel worse. You want to keep some dignity while in so much pain. So tell God, in secret. Pull up a chair and have an imaginary conversation with the person, letting all the stuff out. Cry and scream and kick the chair over if you need to. Be real.

Second, let the other person go. In the case of my sister, I could hardly believe she would go ahead and get pregnant when she knew how I'd take it. But, of course, although our lives run parallel, they are not the same. It would only ever be about me having to come to terms with it, not about her avoiding it happening. The jealousy is understandable, but it is not the other person's fault and we mustn't blame anyone else for our pain.

Third, do feel free to avoid meeting that person for now. That extends to places you usually go that might cause you problems: give them a miss if you can. The playground was horrible for me. It was full of prams and baby bumps when all I wanted to do was keep my head down and collect my son. Keeping my social interactions to a small handful of friends who understood really helped.

If contact is unavoidable, keep it to a safe minimum. When my niece was born, I was in bits but knew that I had to go to see her straight away, otherwise I would never be able to face it. We made an eight-hour round trip to spend an hour with them. When we arrived and I saw the baby asleep in the pram, I no sooner took one look than I was stumbling towards the bathroom and bawling my eyes out. I had avoided babies for months, if not years, and this was the first time I had been close to one. It was heart-wrenching agony, but I did it. I made a decision to feel proud of myself and to be glad for my sister. It also made the next time a tiny bit easier.

Response

Try writing your feelings down so they don't build up and explode as an angry outburst. Practise forgiveness – again! Forgive those who hurt you simply by seeming to live their lives so easily. Turn to God again in the stillness and ask him for his help. Jealousy can keep you focused on your own lack, and others' plenty, so remind yourself of the good things in your life to help restore the balance.

Lord, all I can focus on sometimes is the gaping hole in my life where my baby should be. It feels as though everyone else just gets what they want. I can't stand it. You have said in your word that your grace is enough. Please show me how that is possible.
Amen.

_____

_____

_____

_____

_____

_____

_____

_____

_____

_____

_____

_____

_____

_____

Day 21

Psalm 42

I long to drink of you, O God,
drinking deeply from the streams of pleasure
flowing from your presence.
My longings overwhelm me for more of you!
My soul thirsts, pants, and longs for the living God.
I want to come and see the face of God.
Day and night my tears keep falling
and my heart keeps crying for your help
while my enemies mock me over and over, saying,
'Where is this God of yours? Why doesn't he help you?'
So I speak over my heartbroken soul,
'Take courage. Remember when you used to be
right out in front leading the procession of praise
when the great crowd of worshippers
gathered to go into the presence of the Lord?
You shouted with joy as the sound of passionate celebration
filled the air and the joyous multitude of lovers
honored the festival of the Lord!'
So then, my soul, why would you be depressed?
Why would you sink into despair?
Just keep hoping and waiting on God, your Savior.
For no matter what, I will still sing with praise,
for living before his face is my saving grace!

Psalm 42

Here I am depressed and downcast.
Yet I will still remember you as I ponder the place
where your glory streams down from the mighty mountaintops,
lofty and majestic – the mountains of your awesome presence.
My deep need calls out to the deep kindness of your love.
Your waterfalls of weeping sent waves of sorrow
over my soul, carrying me away,
cascading over me like a thundering cataract.
Yet all day long God's promises of love pour over me.
Through the night I sing his songs,
for my prayer to God has become my life.
I will say to God, 'You are my mountain of strength;
how could you forget me?
Why must I suffer this vile oppression of my enemies –
these heartless tormentors who are out to kill me?'
Their wounding words pierce my heart
over and over while they say,
'Where is this God of yours?'
So I say to my soul,
'Don't be discouraged. Don't be disturbed.
For I know my God will break through for me.'
Then I'll have plenty of reasons to praise him all over again.
Yes, living before his face is my saving grace!

(TPT)

Response

_____

_____

_____

_____

Day 22

Morning glory

Do you know the plant ipomoea? Going by the popular name of morning glory, it is a climber, covering trellises and fences with its spread of leaves and sensational flowers. I had never seen one until the summer after my first two miscarriages, when my mother-in-law began growing one in her garden. Immediately, it became the symbol for my lost children, demonstrating death and hope within its blooms.

You see, each flower lasts for only one day. In the morning it opens blue with a soft yellow centre, and as the day goes on its colours change, becoming more vividly bright pink, until sunset when it closes for the first and final time. Its loss seems wrong: premature, unnecessary, when its life seemed so increasingly vibrant. But look at the vine again and you will see buds, lots of them, appearing as twisted coils ready to unfurl their day-long majesty before too long.

My children had lasted for only a short time. No one had ever seen them to witness just how spectacular they were going to be. In a blink, they were gone. There really is something so horribly abrupt about miscarriage. Their actual existence was momentary, their potential only to be guessed at.

I planted a morning glory the following spring. By then I had lost a further child and the plant's symbolism felt even more poignant. As the colours developed during each day, my heart would ache for the beauty and the futility of it. Why would this bud, looking like a coiled spring the previous day, put so much effort into its appearance? Why would it bother intensifying in colour, becoming more attractive to the garden visitor as each hour passed, when it knew how short its duration would be?

For me, part of the answer to that question is that life – however brief – is always worth dressing up for. Jesus asks the crowd whether a single sparrow falls to the ground without its Father in heaven noticing. A sparrow – commonplace and not the most handsome of birds – nevertheless gets heaven's attention when it dies. How much more your little one?

How much potential for glory was there in him or her? We can only guess. But how much glory was there in their actual existence – the days or weeks of life? The morning glory plant tells me that their beauty was breathtaking; the sort you can't take your eyes off. Oh, I know you long to have seen your baby through your own eyes, and the pain of not having done so is unbearable at times. But they were real. As important to creation as those who live to be a hundred. And just as glorious.

Response

Jesus, I've been so caught up in what 'should have been' that I've missed the truth of what my baby actually is: perfect, beautiful, and in your care. Please comfort me with that thought today.

_____

_____

_____

_____

_____

_____

_____

_____

_____

_____

Morning glory

_____

_____

_____

_____

_____

_____

_____

_____

_____

_____

_____

_____

_____

_____

Day 23

Mother's Day

I've always thought that Mother's Day can be a bitter-sweet occasion at the best of times. Although none of us would exist without a mother, not all of us continue through life at her side. Whether through death or estrangement, many do not have the relationship with their mother that their soul craves, and when the cards start appearing in the shops (about two months before the date itself), it can be a painful reminder of what is missing.

I have happy memories of Mother's Day when I was a child. My mum would be sure to be in church – not her usual habit at that stage of her life – and us four children would traipse up to the front at the appointed moment to collect a small bunch of daffodils held together by an elastic band. These were pressed proudly into my mother's hand before we took our seat on the unyielding wooden pews to continue the rest of the service. That simple act of giving a bunch of flowers was so special to me: I knew I was making my mum happy but was aware that it created a connection that touched something within myself, too.

If this were a movie, there would be a sound at this point like a needle being dragged across a vinyl LP. Fast forward to Mother's Day as seen through the eyes not of someone who has no mother but of a mother who has no child: not just bitter-sweet but excruciating. When I was miscarrying, watching all those children eagerly collecting their flowers or chocolate to give to their smiling mummies, it felt as if I was the only person in the world not invited to Christmas.

If I had felt more reasonable about it, perhaps I could have sat there hugging the secret to myself of knowing I was a mother even though my children had never been born. Technically, it may have been possible to do that; but I had no more control of my emotions than a juggernaut hurtling down a hill with no brakes. To be honest, I hated the tableau of 'perfect' family life that was literally parading through the church. I couldn't bear it, and I either sobbed my way through the ordeal or avoided going altogether.

Now, I'm the first one to admit that a platitude delivered at a terrible time is an awful thing. Soundbites do not tend to bring healing to difficult situations. However, I will pass on something that was said to me kindly, well-meaningly, one Mother's Day. 'Just because you have never held your baby in your arms does not mean you are not a mother.'

Hear that again. 'Just because you have never held your baby in your arms does not mean you are not a mother.' Even if this is horribly small comfort, let it be the little comfort that it is. It is not a case of 'mind over matter', of trying to reframe a situation to make ourselves feel better. It is a real truth that we are mothers – broken and grieving what is missing – but mothers nonetheless.

At our church, the children hand out chocolates on Mother's Day to all the ladies present as a way of including everyone who might have loved to be a mother if they'd had the chance. It's a simple gesture, but one that unites rather than divides. It stops the day being about winners and losers, the haves and the have nots. And in any case, it's a great excuse for some chocolate.

Response

Make a point of going out today and buying yourself your favourite chocolate. Find a nice place where you can sit and savour every mouthful of it. Cry if you need to, smile if you can. Surrender the moment to God, giving thanks again for your little one and the gift they have been to your life. You know that if they were here right now they would be showering you with their love – and wanting to pinch some of the chocolate. Stay in that place until you have sensed their presence in your heart and feel strong enough to face the rest of the day.

_____

_____

_____

_____

_____

_____

_____

_____

_____

_____

_____

_____

_____

Day 24

It takes two

So, you were going to be parents! A shared adventure! Having a baby was going to cement the two of you together like nothing else could. If you already have a child, this baby was going to complete you, or at least expand you. The world seemed a bigger place, somehow; and it was yours to conquer. But then it went wrong and, like most of life's problems, it made a lot of other things go wrong as well.

Don't be surprised if your relationship is put under strain. One of the most common things I hear from women after miscarriage is that they feel they've lost their partner too. As if it wasn't bad enough already! Just when you need to lean on him, for him to be your rock, it seems he's crumbled – that is, if you can find him . . .

When trouble hits, a man needs time to regroup and he does this most effectively on his own. For us women, it affects us badly twice. We have the problem itself, and on top of that we have an absent or distant partner. I don't know about you, but when it happens to me it feels like a terrible rejection. The ache in a woman's heart is best relieved by human contact – whether that's touch, or just being able to talk – and our man is the one we crave the most. For the most part, men don't seem to understand that we need these simple things.

Don't be surprised, either, if you find yourself arguing more. Some of that will be the anger and tiredness and hormones, but some will be your way of trying to demand attention. On his part, he will be feeling totally helpless. He couldn't stop the miscarriage any more than you could, but the unbearable thing for him is that he can't seem to make you better either. By nature, man is a problem-solver, a fixer. And no one can fix this.

If it seems he is over it, that he has managed to move on, then remember that appearances are deceptive. The fact is, his response to all this is going to be different from yours. You felt the baby within you. Your body had already undergone the process of change, of preparation. To your partner, you may have looked the same as normal, if your miscarriage was early. After the loss, in his eyes you may just be the original normal – your body looks unchanged, like nothing happened. That isn't heartless on his part; remember, you didn't look pregnant to most of the people around you, either.

You and God are the ones who really know! You felt the evidence of your baby's existence; while God actually saw him or her from the moment fertilization occurred. But he is the one who also put you together with your partner, watched you fall in love, and put the desire for each other within you.

I wonder if you had this reading at your marriage service?

> Two are better than one,
> because they have a good return for their labour;
> If either of them falls down,
> one can help the other up.
> But pity anyone who falls
> and has no one to help them up.
> Also, if two lie down together, they will keep warm.
> But how can one keep warm alone?
> Though one may be overpowered,
> two can defend themselves.
> A cord of three strands is not quickly broken.
> (Ecclesiastes 4.9–12, NIV 2011)

Along with the promises to do with 'for better or for worse', these verses might have been glossed over back then; but they are starting to become highly significant now at this troubled time. In the normal ups and downs of married life, it is usually the case that you 'fall over' one at a time, the one still standing free to help the other up. After miscarriage, you have both fallen. Your attempts at trying to help your partner can leave you weaker from the effort, and you're both still on the floor.

So, what about the three-cord strand? It's time to call on the third member of your marriage: God himself. He sees you both laid out, as helpless as a beetle on its back. He is the one who has the strength to raise you up and then hold you tight while you recover.

Response

Spend some time in prayer for yourself and your partner. If you feel that you have blamed him, or made him the enemy, it would be helpful to ask God to help you forgive him. It would also be good if you were able to pray together; but, in any case, be sure to pray.

Lord, thank you for _____. Thank you for all the love we have shared up until now, and for our baby that we created together. Help us to get through this together. Help me to be gentle with him and to be able to explain how it is for me. Help him to find the words to tell me how he's feeling, too.

We can't do this without you, God. It's testing us to the point of breaking. Please give us the strength we need and help us love each other better. Amen.

_____

_____

_____

Day 25

Job's comforters

————◆◆————

'You've got a friend in me.' 'Thank you for being a friend.' 'I'll be there for you.'

TV programmes and films often bring home the message that we need friends to see us through life. I hope you have a group of friends and family around you to help at this difficult time. But, strange though it may sound, there will be days when you wish you were alone! Why? Because sometimes it is the well-meaning but way-off-course help that is hardest to bear.

In the book of Job we read how the best attempts of Job's friends to comfort him in his suffering fall wide of the mark. Taken on their own, some of their comments do contain truth and lead towards God. And I suppose, to be fair to them, they were attempting the impossible: to explain things about God that are designed to be unexplained and cloaked in mystery. We are not God, however much we want to be in charge! That is both reassuring and intensely annoying. We feel unable to continue on the journey until we know why we're not getting to where we want to go. Sometimes it is the right path, but it meanders and twists and hides its endpoint, and in the meantime we've practically given up even moving.

I always feel a bit sorry for Job's comforters. They were basing their ideas on the story in front of them, without being able to read the preface. We read in chapter 1 that Satan was behind Job's afflictions. There is never the suggestion that he'd been chosen because he harboured sin, practised injustice or was in any way hypocritical about his walk with God. In fact, the Bible makes clear that his suffering was a direct assault against his uprightness and exemplary life (Job 1.8: 'Then the LORD said to Satan, "Have you considered my servant Job? There is no one on earth like him; he is blameless and upright, a man who fears God and shuns evil"'). So when they trot out the clichés about how this must somehow be his fault, it adds more pain to an already unbearable situation.

I had a 'Job's comforter'. This friend didn't mean to get it wrong, and there were times when she truly managed to help. She came to visit often and we would talk and cry and pray. However, on one particular day she brought more harm than healing. Around the same time that I miscarried there were two other pregnant ladies in the church. One sailed through in textbook fashion, but recently the other had begun to bleed and was put on bed-rest. After a couple of weeks the danger was over and all was well. While I wouldn't have wished a miscarriage on anyone, it was really hard to swallow the fact that it looked as though my prayers hadn't been answered but this lady's had.

My friend went on to describe in some detail how this lady had prayed in a particular way. I tried to challenge what she was saying, and in turn my friend tried to back-pedal, but I was heartbroken. Not only was I going through the agony of wondering if there was something wrong with my body – in fact with me, full stop – but now I was being told I wasn't even praying right! Yet again, I felt the crushing weight of blame; I had failed to prevent my miscarriage because I didn't use the right words.

When you are having a miscarriage, in the moments when everything is being shaken and fear is at its greatest, do you think God is standing over you, judging your prayer life? If you were drowning, would the lifeboat crew refuse to pluck you from the waves because the emergency phone call was not worded correctly? What rubbish! Even if the air was blue with expletives, they would focus all their expertise on getting the rescue completed. So it is with our loving Father God. Goodness, kindness and unconditional love are who he is, not just what he does.

Can I gently suggest that you ask for wisdom with regard to your friendships at the moment? It might be the case that the best friend for you right now is one who has been on the fringes; that the one you thought was your best friend isn't quite right for this situation. No one will get it right with you every time, but keep a look out for the one who makes you feel better.

Response

Jesus, thank you that you call us your friends. I'm not a very good friend myself at the moment, but I really need some friends in my life to help me through all this.

Show me who I should turn to. Help me deal with the ones who hurt me by their insensitive comments. Help me forgive them, Lord. I don't want to lose friends. I pray that, when I come through a lot of this, there will be friendships waiting for me on the other side.

Amen.

_____

_____

_____

_____

_____

_____

_____

_____

_____

_____

_____

_____

_____

Day 26

Due date

———◆———

I bet the moment you knew you were pregnant, you went over to the calendar or pulled out your diary and made a note of the due date. Some of you will have spent the months you were trying to conceive with a potential due date in mind. 'Just before Christmas!' or 'A summer baby, won't that be lovely!' While inside you the cells are dividing and only just beginning to form your baby, on the outside you've practically hung up the bunting.

What on earth are we supposed to do now the arrival has been cancelled? Our complete focus was on a particular day that would bring wonderful joy. Now all that's left is a day we dread.

This is yet one more thing to grieve over and process. Nothing is straightforward here, as you well know by now, and what should have been your baby's birthday can never be just another day. It is made all the harder when a friend or relative, or someone you work with, is expecting at about the same time as you. Every single time you see them, you won't be able to help comparing their situation with yours. The cry 'It should have been me!' is well justified. It really should have been you.

Don't try to talk yourself out of the way you feel. Put it this way: even though it is years since some of my relatives passed away, I still think of them on what was their special day. I can no longer celebrate with them, but they – and their birthday – are never forgotten; although that is a very different situation, of course.

Due date

If you suffered a late miscarriage, you may be torn between whether to commemorate their birthday or their due date. If it helps, I would go for their birthday. Focusing on when they should have been born may well add too much pain.

Many women ask how they are supposed to mark their baby's due date. Some choose to go to work as usual, to keep busy and try to block it out. Others embrace it as a day of remembrance and choose special activities to mark the occasion. There is no right and wrong way. It will depend on you and what's best for your situation.

The actual due date was the hardest for me. By then, months had gone past and not a single friend or relative could have told me when I'd been due. I felt I was the only one who cared. As the day approached, I could see where I'd circled the date in the diary. Despite the miscarriage, I couldn't bring myself to rub it out, and so there it was as I turned the page. I spent time in reflection, shed some tears, but did nothing else. Yet again, it was a private, lonely grief. I felt hollow and didn't quite know how to fill the void.

We began this book on Day 1 with the statement 'My baby was real'. I wonder if you are able – if not now, then at some point in the future – to think of your baby as present with you today, rather than absent? The longing to hold them is unbearable, but they are real; lodged in your heart and in your thoughts. Try to put away the sense of what isn't, and hold dearly to what is: the sure knowledge that you are a mother on your child's birthday.

If you choose to mark it, here are some suggestions.

- If you have your baby's ashes, it would be a good time to scatter or bury them – if you can face parting with them. There will be a place of great significance for you that will be the perfect spot. It might be somewhere you can visit often, or somewhere you have had special holidays and can make a bigger thing of in the future.
- Light a candle. Sadly, our babies will never blow out the ones on their birthday cakes. As you watch the flame flicker, it is a reminder of the

fragility of life; but you will be warmed by it, too. Moments like this are always bitter-sweet, a sad beauty. Be conscious of the presence of Jesus, if you can. In calling himself the Light of the World, he comes to dispel darkness. This season is indeed very dark, and the smallest light can lift the gloom.

- Release a balloon. If you have other children, they can each have one for the brother or sister they didn't get to meet. Again, pick a place that is special to your family. You may want to say a prayer or some kind of tribute to your little one before letting go of the string. Keep watching the balloon as it weaves its way upwards, buffeted by the wind currents.
- Go out for the day or go on a date in the evening. Talk about your baby as much as you need to, then move the conversation on if you can to find good in the present. So much of what we suffer, we suffer alone. On this day of all days, aim to reconnect with your partner.

It does get better, you know. I find I no longer need to recall the due dates, but if you do then that's fine. It's not that those days don't matter, just that over time the 'missing them' becomes more generalized. I truly feel that they are part of me every day, and will be until I finally have them in my arms.

Response

Write down some of your ideas for marking your baby's due date. Talk them over with whoever you want to share the day with. Having something positive to focus on will be really helpful as the day approaches. Write it on your calendar and pray that God blesses your plans.

_____

_____

_____

_____

Due date

_____

_____

_____

_____

_____

_____

_____

_____

_____

_____

_____

_____

_____

Day 27

Always something to remind me

As we go through life we find that there are some things we would love to forget, some that are impossible to forget, and some we vow to remember always. No matter how long it has been since your miscarriage – days, weeks, months or years – you know that it stays with you.

You've probably found out by now that most people seem to assume you can draw a line under it: dust yourself off and move on. The fact is, it is impossible to forget our lost babies. Even in their absence, they are part of our everyday. But sometimes it is helpful to have something physical as a reminder. You may have a scan photo, or even a photo of your delivered baby. But for many of us there is nothing: no evidence that they were there, only that they were gone. You may have already chosen to commemorate your baby in some way; but if you haven't, I would like to encourage you to do so.

In the Old Testament, there are several examples of God telling his people to set up a memorial to mark a significant occasion. Not only would this remind them of what had happened, and how God had helped them, but future generations would ask, 'What is the meaning behind this memorial?' It was a way of keeping their attention on what was still important.

When a person has lived out their life, it is usually the headstone that stands as a memorial. Being able to leave flowers there on significant dates is a way of honouring those we have loved and lost. Sadly, many miscarriages happen too soon for the babies to have this done for them; but in any case, we don't want to only think of them as gone. They are with us all the time in our hearts, and it seems better to me that we remember them as somehow living.

There are many different ways you could do this; I would like to offer some suggestions for what to use as a memorial.

- A piece of jewellery. In the description of the priestly garments in Exodus 39.6–7, we read, 'They mounted the onyx stones in gold filigree settings and engraved them like a seal with the names of the sons of Israel. Then they fastened them on the shoulder pieces of the ephod as memorial stones for the sons of Israel.' I love that this is proof that the sons of Israel were something precious and beautiful. You don't need to choose something expensive, but a necklace that hangs near your heart or a ring on your finger is a constant reminder of your baby. After my third miscarriage, I bought a Russian wedding ring, with its three bands interlinked. It seemed a lovely way of showing that they were always together.
- A tattoo. This wouldn't be everyone's choice, but to have your baby's name, or a pair of footprints, engraved on your body is a permanent reminder. Choose a place that can be seen if you want to invite comment, or hidden if you don't.
- If your baby was miscarried late, it may be possible to have casts made of his or her feet and hands. Set in plaster within a frame, it is the closest thing to touching them.
- Put together a treasure box, if appropriate. Include a copy of a newspaper for the day they were lost and of the day they would have been born. If you received any presents or had bought items yourself, pop these in as well.
- Plant something in your garden. A tree is the ideal choice, but only if you plan to stay put: it would be difficult to move away and leave it behind. A flowering shrub can be taken with you if necessary, and will give years of poignant pleasure. Some roses have significant names, such as Sweet Child of Mine, Blessings, Remember Me and Scent from Heaven.

- As I suggested yesterday, light candles on memorial days, the baby's birthday, or the day they were lost.

Response

Can a mother forget the baby at her breast and have no compassion on the child she has borne? . . . I will not forget you! See I have engraved you on the palms of my hands.

(Isaiah 49.15–16)

Lord, once more I thank you for my baby. I cannot forget him/her and would never do so! Please show me which form of commemoration would bring me most comfort as a reminder of my baby.
Amen.

Day 28

Psalm 116

———◆◆◆———

I am passionately in love with God because he listens to me.
He hears my prayers and answers them.
As long as I live I'll keep praying to him,
for he stoops down to listen to my heart's cry.
Death once stared me in the face,
and I was so close to slipping into its dark shadows.
I was terrified and overcome with sorrow.
I cried out to the Lord, 'God, come and save me!'
He was so kind, so gracious to me.
Because of his passion toward me,
he made everything right and he restored me.
So I've learned from my experience
that God protects the childlike and humble ones.
For I was broken and brought low,
but he answered me and came to my rescue!
Now I can say to myself and to all,
'Relax and rest, be confident and serene,
for the Lord rewards fully those who simply trust in him.'
God has rescued my soul from death's fear
and dried my eyes of many tears.
He's kept my feet firmly on his path
and strengthened me so that I may please him
and live my life before him in his life-giving light!

Even when it seems I'm surrounded
by many liars and my own fears,
and though I'm hurting in my suffering and trauma,
I still stay faithful to God and speak words of faith.
So now, what can I ever give back to God
to repay him for the blessings he's poured out on me?
I will lift up his cup of salvation and praise him extravagantly
for all he's done for me.
I will fulfil the promise I made to God
in the presence of his gathered people.
When one of God's holy lovers dies,
it is costly to the Lord, touching his heart.
Lord, because I am your loving servant
you have broken open my heart and freed me from my chains.
Now I'll worship you passionately and bring to you
my sacrifice of praise, drenched with thanksgiving!
I'll keep my promise to you, God,
in the presence of your gathered people, just like I said I would.
I will worship you here in your living presence,
in the temple in Jerusalem.
I will worship and sing hallelujah, for I praise you, Lord!

(TPT)

Response

Day 29

Hoping for a rainbow

You will probably have heard the term 'rainbow baby': the baby born after miscarriage. It's different for everyone, but most women I know have wanted to try to conceive again as soon as possible after a miscarriage. Let's face it, the urge to have a baby is what led you to this point in the first place, and it won't have gone away completely. For some, it becomes even more urgent: the sense of time being wasted when you should be having children, the primeval need to fill the emptiness.

Medical opinion varies, and our bodies recover at different rates. If there were no complications, your periods should start up again fairly quickly. Your doctor will advise whether you can 'go for it' straight away, or whether you should let a couple of cycles go by. Many women find that it takes a while for their natural cycle to re-establish, in which case you have to kind of sit it out. But never mind the physical process, I think a fair amount of healing has to take place in the emotions, too.

You will need enormous courage to try again. You now know that the risk of miscarriage is more than a quoted statistic. You are part of the 1-in-4 group. You don't know whether your next pregnancy will be successful. You need to be realistic as well as hopeful. Are you in a strong enough state, mentally and emotionally, to face it all?

I found it quite difficult to conceive each time – probably part of the hormonal problem that was causing the miscarriages anyway. My periods tended to be a bit erratic, so I could never be quite sure when I was ovulating. But by far the biggest obstacle was what was going on in my head and heart.

By the time I had miscarried twice, I had a strong feeling that it would happen again. As it turned out, my third miscarriage was the hardest, medically. I had tried to manage at home, but became quite weak with blood loss and ended up in hospital for several days. It was hideous. I was treated very badly; only the scan radiologist who broke the official news of my loss showed any compassion and care. When the consultant came to see me on the ward, he just said, 'I'd like to see you in my clinic.' I had 'scored' three miscarriages – the most horrible success in the world – and I was through to the next round.

I didn't expect to miscarry a fourth time. I went into that pregnancy with a ridiculous amount of hope. Even though I knew the odds were stacked against me, I felt a joy bubble up inside. I told more people, so they could pray. I felt protected medically and socially. When I miscarried, I found myself in hospital sharing a bay with two ladies who were booked in for sterilizations the next day. They talked carelessly about the prospect of never having to worry about contraception again. I pulled the curtains around my bed and cried silently.

It was probably the lowest point in the whole process for me. So many prayers had gone up, so many tests and investigations had been done, and I'd even received some treatment; and it had all amounted to nothing. I gave up all hope and began to think that adoption was the only way forward. I had no strength to face another loss. I'd had enough of the pain and loneliness. I simply had no resources left. I was done. But my family wasn't complete and the hunger to have another baby of my own never left.

It was like when you're on a long walk and you find that you're lost. The map makes no sense. You've missed a turn somewhere and now you could be anywhere; but you need to get back to the car park, need to get home. The choice is always: do you go back and try to retrace your steps, or do you bash on, trusting there'll be another path somewhere that will set you right again? I found myself looking back at the four miscarriages and wondering what they had been for. If I gave up now, what was the point of all that? But if I could somehow press on, find the strength and courage and have my 'rainbow baby', then their losses would have been worth something.

Into this heart-searching came these verses from Romans 4.18–21 that I began to cling to:

> Against all hope, Abraham in hope believed and so became the father of many nations, just as it had been said to him, 'So shall your offspring be.' Without weakening in his faith, he faced the fact his body was as good as dead . . . and that Sarah's womb was also dead. Yet he did not waver through unbelief regarding the promise of God, but was strengthened in his faith and gave glory to God, being fully persuaded that God had power to do what he had promised.

When I prayed originally about whether to start a family I had these words from Isaiah 54.13: 'All your sons will be taught by the LORD and great will be your children's peace.' I believed at that moment that I would have sons – plural. Could I still trust God to fulfil his promise to me, after so many disappointments? I realized I had to decide. Either God meant what he said or he didn't. If he didn't, then he was a liar and a tease, and not who I thought him to be. But if I trusted him, called myself his child, then surely I had to believe that he spoke the truth? And that meant that despite all the evidence to the contrary God was still able to give me the son he promised me.

It was faith that won out for me. Not reason, not psyching myself up, not believing that medical intervention would overrule, just plain choosing to believe God. I would quote the Romans verses every day, believing that the words would take root in my heart and do their job. I asked God to give me hope, because I had none.

Did Hannah have hope when she went into the Temple and pleaded with God to give her a child? (You can read her story in 1 Samuel chapter 1.) She certainly had desperation. I think that counts sometimes. God promises to give us the desires of our hearts. A woman cannot shake off the desire to have a baby. When she's got it, she's got it bad. So when well-meaning friends suggest that you should give up, even when you're at your lowest ebb your heart can't quite do it.

How do we know when to keep trying and when to stop? Some will have no choice. An emergency hysterectomy has to be done. Menopause arrives. A partner leaves. All these situations need careful handling, and each requires you to go through a grief process.

But if you are still physically able to conceive, what next?

I don't have the answers, any more than you do. We have to make our own decisions. But we need to hear from God, don't we? Without him, we are in danger of wandering off, getting ourselves into more trouble. In any matter where guidance is required, I find peace to be the thing that shows me if I'm right. You see, I was ready to give up; in fact, I had. But in time, I found myself challenged and uncomfortable about that decision. It had felt the right one to make, but under God's spotlight I could see it differently. My will had to change, again, until it was in line with his, and peace returned. He called me towards the scary step of trying again.

This may not be the same for you. Perhaps he might be saying to stop trying; to leave it to him; to let him satisfy your heart in other ways. It takes faith, either way. We have to believe he has the best for us. That's what it all boils down to in the end. We need to be so surrendered to him that all we want at the end of the rainbow is him.

Response

Father, this is scary for me: to ask you if I should try again or not. I'm worried that you'll give me the wrong answer or you won't answer at all. Please give me more faith and help me trust that you've got the very best plans for my life. Please make sense of everything I've already been through and give me your peace. Help me to say, like Jesus did, 'Your will be done.'

_____

_____

_____

_____

_____

_____

_____

_____

_____

_____

_____

_____

_____

Day 30

The end of the road

It's our last day together. For the last month, we have walked hand in hand through this section of your journey through miscarriage. It is my fervent hope that your heart has been comforted and that your steps have grown a little stronger. We both know it's not the end, but merely another fork in the path. Truthfully, this particular road will keep on going; but it won't always feel so difficult to tread.

In the process of grief, the final step is acceptance. A similar word is resignation, but there is a powerful difference between them. Resignation implies giving up, or at least giving in. Shrugging your shoulders and allowing yourself to be bowed down by the weight of it. Acceptance, however, is a mature stage to be in. It means that you have faced it all down, stared at it long and hard, and have said, 'It is well with my soul.'

Acceptance will mean different things to each of us. It will also include a whole range of topics, some of which are relatively easy to accept, others much more painfully difficult.

I accept that:

- My baby died against my will.
- I can never think about my baby without some measure of sadness or regret.
- For now, and for however long, I am not pregnant.

- I do not know when, or if ever, I will become pregnant again.
- This is the shape of my life for now.
- Other people around me will be having babies while I am not.

The 'speaking it out by faith' kind of list might look like this.
  I accept that:

- My baby is safe in the arms of my Father God.
- My baby will never know any harm or pain.
- God has my very best interests at heart. His plans are not to hurt me but to prosper me.
- My family looks like it does for now, and God places us in families to bless us.

The biggest benefit of reaching the point of acceptance is the peace that it brings. Miscarriage is a place of trauma, grief and despair. No one can survive in that emotional state indefinitely. The cause and source of it might remain, but our reactions and responses can change if time and space are allowed. When you can read through those lists and agree with most of them, you will be in a place of greater peace than at the start.

Being a Christian has wonderful upsides, but difficult downsides. When life is sweet, we declare ourselves blessed and favoured. God loves us! All is right with the world! But when trouble hits we have to be able to say, with as much conviction, that God loves us even when all is not right with the world. That takes faith. It takes the decision to believe that God is all he says he is, when he seems to be acting in our lives in ways that contradict it.

At its heart, the message of suffering is that God 'gives and he takes away, blessed be the name of the Lord'. That has never gone far enough for me. It is too trite, too simplistic, and takes no account of how we might be feeling. I do, however, believe in its truth: that God is in charge; we do not always understand, but we can always count on his love.

A great verse of acceptance for me is Psalm 16.6: 'The boundary lines have fallen for me in pleasant places; surely I have a delightful inheritance.' Believe you me, there are times I have spoken out this verse when my surroundings have been terrible! I have thanked God through gritted teeth and with tears rolling down my cheeks. Do you know those words in 1 Thessalonians 5.18 about thanking God in all circumstances? Although this can be the hardest thing to do, it can release something in us that we wouldn't expect: in among everything else is a whisper of peace. I feel my shoulders relax and my breathing settle. I'm reminding myself that God knows best. He promises in Psalm 23 that he will make me lie down in green pastures. Well, even if that green pasture contains a mere half dozen blades of grass, I choose to trust him, to believe that lying here for a while is the best thing for me.

Throughout this book, I have wanted to point you to Jesus – the one you might have some issues with, but the one you need more than oxygen. He has shown me what it is like to pursue a faithful life in the midst of suffering. Hebrews 12.2 reminds us that 'for the joy set before him [Jesus] endured the cross . . . and sat down at the right hand of the throne of God'. Jesus went through terrible suffering but somehow found joy in accepting it.

Wouldn't that be great? To find some joy and peace where we find ourselves? This is my prayer for you as you continue on this journey.

Dear Lord,
I pray for every person reading this book that you have met them in its pages. Comfort them with your love. Reassure them that you love them completely. Keep their babies in your care until the day they are reunited. Heal them, Lord. Lighten the weight in their hearts.

Restore their strained and broken relationships. Bring them out the other side with compassion and tenderness.
For Jesus' sake,
Amen.

Response

_____

_____

_____

_____

_____

_____

_____

_____

_____

_____

_____

_____

_____

_____

Liturgy for saying goodbye

In the absence of a funeral, our baby's passing may slip away unnoticed, unmarked. Even though you may have followed some of the suggestions for memorial in Day 27, there may still be a sense that things are left incomplete.

In this section, I have offered a pattern you may wish to follow as a ceremony of farewell for your child. This can be as private as you like – you may even conduct this on your own – but it can provide an opportunity to come together with those near to you who have lost their grandchild, niece or nephew, or cousin.

Choose the day carefully. You will want enough time to have passed to be healed physically and to have regained your strength; but don't wait so long that it seems unreal. Make sure that the people you need to be there are able to come – this is not a time for further disappointment. If your guests want to bring a present, let them. However poignant and difficult now, at some point in the future all of these tokens will mean a great deal.

The time of day may have significance, too. In the daytime, while the sun is still up, there is the reminder of hope, light and warmth. At dusk, as the sun is setting, nature is providing its own farewell.

Whether to hold the ceremony outside or indoors is your choice; there is no right or wrong. Outdoors, you may sense a connection with nature itself and her passing seasons. Inside is your home, the place where your baby belongs.

Take whatever items best represent your child. Light your candles, blow up your balloons, hold the soft toy. Gather together, united in grief and love, and – with courage in your hearts – begin.

Liturgy for saying goodbye

We meet together today to give thanks to God for the life of our child
_____ [*name the baby where appropriate*].

Although the world may not have noticed *him/her* arrive or slip away,
although we may never have seen *him/her*,
together, we acknowledge our love for *him/her*.

We pray that *he/she* be kept safe in your hands, God, and that you will
hold *him/her* on our behalf until that day comes when we are together.

In losing our baby, we have lost our hopes and dreams. All of the loss
has left us empty. We ask for your love to fill us again, Lord.

The Bible says, blessed are those who mourn, for they will be comforted. So, we ask for your comfort, God. We ask for strength and
courage as we walk this path of pain. We choose to place our hand in
yours, trusting that you know best. Keep leading us forward into hope.

*The following poem by Christy Kenneally can be read, along with other
contributions from those gathered:*

> DEAR PARENTS
> I did not die young.
> I lived my span of life,
> Within your body
> And within your love.
>
> There are many
> Who have lived long lives
> And have not been loved as me.

Liturgy for saying goodbye

If you would honour me
Then speak my name
And number me among your family.

If you would honour me.
Then strive to live in love
For in that love, I live.

Never ever doubt
That we will meet again.

Until that happy day,
I will grow with God
And wait for you.

To conclude, say the Lord's Prayer:

Our Father in heaven,
Hallowed be your name,
Your kingdom come,
Your will be done
On earth as in heaven.
Give us today our daily bread
And forgive us our sins
As we forgive those who sin against us.
Lead us not into temptation
But deliver us from evil.
For the kingdom, the power and the glory are yours
Now and for ever,
Amen.

Resources

For advice and support:

Baby Loss
www.babyloss.com
Lists regional support groups in the UK.

Miscarriage Association
Email: info@miscarriageassociation.org.uk
Helpline: 01924 200 799 (Monday to Friday 9 a.m. to 4 p.m.)

NCT
www.nct.org.uk/pregnancy/miscarriage-support

Open
A ministry of CARE (Christian Action Research and Education).
www.weareopen.org.uk
Email: open@care.org.uk

SANDS
www.sands.org.uk

Additionally, many of the general childcare support sites such as <www.netmums.com> carry threads and forums on the subject.

Bible acknowledgements